The Ultimate Guide to
Running with Your Dog

The Ultimate Guide to Running with Your Dog

Tips and Techniques for Understanding Your Canine's Fitness and Running Temperament

BRYAN BARRERA

Skyhorse Publishing

Skyhorse Publishing books may be purchased in bulk at special discounts for sales promotion, corporate gifts, fund-raising, or educational purposes. Special editions can also be created to specifications. For details, contact the Special Sales Department, Skyhorse Publishing, 307 West 36th Street, 11th Floor, New York, NY 10018 or info@skyhorsepublishing.com.

Skyhorse® and Skyhorse Publishing® are registered trademarks of Skyhorse Publishing, Inc.®, a Delaware corporation.

Visit our website at www.skyhorsepublishing.com.

10 9 8 7 6 5 4 3 2 1

Library of Congress Cataloging-in-Publication Data is available on file.

Cover design by Tom Lau

Print ISBN: 978-1-5107-5070-8
Ebook ISBN: 978-1-5107-5877-3

Printed in China

Photo by Chris Roden

ACKNOWLEDGEMENTS

Thank you to my wife, Suzanne, for taking on an even heavier workload with our home, family, and company while I pursued this project. Without you, none of this is possible.

Thank you to my mother, Cynthia, for your words of encouragement and unwavering support on the many midnight calls.

Thank you to Chris Roden and Nick Wignall for the stunning photography that brought this book to life.

Thank you to all the runners who have helped DC Dog Runner. Your contributions, both large and small, have helped shape our culture. Thank you to the families that have allowed us to spend time with your dogs. It is because of you that I enjoy every day of work!

Thank you to the University of Dallas; you turned me into a writer after all!

And finally, thank you to the incredible team at Skyhorse Publishing. To editors Veronica Alvarado for approaching me about the project and helping me in the early stages of writing, to Yezanira Venecia for your patience and diligence, and to Julie Ganz for guiding me through the completion of this project.

The Barrera Family: Bryan, Suzanne, Owen, Phillip, Mary Eloise, Aoife, and Paul

For my grandpa, Pablo O. Barrera.
Thank you for the example of being a good man.
You excelled at being a husband, father, grandfather,
and great-grandfather.
I strive to be a little more like you every day.

Table of Contents

Bryan running with Seamus in Highland Park, Texas.

Photo by Nick Wignall

CHAPTER ONE:
You Do What?

When I tell people that I run dogs for a living, the response generally falls into one of two camps. The first is:

- "That's the most ridiculous thing I've ever heard. Why would anyone hire someone to run their dog?"
- "Why would you get a dog if you can't run with them or spend the time exercising them?"
- "Can't you just throw them a ball?"
- "Do you actually run other people's dogs?"

The questions continue on and on to borderline insult level where I start to question myself!

The second camp being:

- "That's the coolest thing I've ever heard! How do I sign up?"
- "Wait ... you spend your time running with other people's dogs and get paid for it?"
- "I have a crazy dog who has so much energy; do you have a card?"

What it seems to come down to is the following: either you have spent time with a dog that needs to run, or you have not. It really is that simple. If you have not owned a hyperactive dog, or have been fortunate enough to have a dog that is satisfied with their daily dog walks, then I get it; it seems absurd that you would outsource the exercise of your dog. But there is a segment of the population that is at its wit's end trying to find a solution for their dog with endless amounts of energy, aggressiveness, or even destructive behaviors.

I've spoken with families that have spent a lot of time and money trying to solve the problems that eventually lead them to our company. They'll purchase harnesses, specialty collars, and leashes searching for peace of mind and a positive experience outside the home. Tools like those are definitely part of the solution, but like your own health, taking a holistic approach can yield different, and potentially better, results.

I've been operating DC Dog Runner for six years now, with the sole intention of bringing happiness, as well as physical and mental stimulation, to our pets through long-distance running. To the exclusion of all other pet services we can offer, we have chosen to focus on running with dogs for half-hour- and hour-long runs, multiple times a week.

The majority of the dogs we run benefit from and are fully stimulated by the half-hour option. If a dog has not been doing any consistent exercise beyond being let out for the restroom, they can be built up to cover that time over a few weeks. Our approach is to begin with the half-hour-long run as the goal.

The hour-long runs are a bit more breed- or even dog-specific. If we are just filling in for a runner who routinely takes his dog on long-distance runs and we need to maintain the fitness for a dog to keep up, we offer the hour. If the dog is a specific breed like a Vizsla, Weimaraner, German Shorthaired Pointer, etc., with lean, muscular, athletic builds, we recommend the hour. Just like us, the benefits only begin with physical fitness for the dogs. The long-distance running gives them work to do and a sense of purpose.

While it started with me running with dogs in my spare time to have fun and pocket a little extra cash, it has now grown into a small army of fifteen runners. My wife, Suzanne, and I have been able to turn it into one of the best dog-running companies in America, as named by *Runner's World* magazine!

My first appearance in *Runner's World* magazine.

Photograph by Ryan Donnell

How to Use This Book

Consider this a reference guide to running with your dog. The idea is to deliver information I pulled from research and my personal experiences to help you better understand your dog and its needs. Can you read this book cover to cover? Yes, and please do, but you can also use it to look up helpful tips for the specific kind of running you're going to do that may be a little different than your normal routine. That is where this guide is going to be most helpful: whether you are a newbie who just adopted their first overactive dog, or a trail master who is looking for suggestions and solutions to help your current needs. I really hope this book and, more importantly, information can be shared in our running and dog communities to ensure that we are keeping in mind our four-legged friends turned road warriors!

Ideally, you can find everything you need for any situation. Say you'll be running in the city, primarily after work, when it is hot because it is summer. You can navigate smoothly around from topic to topic to piece together all the pertinent information on just those kinds of conditions. Same goes for a rainy, cold, trail run, but this time you are running with multiple dogs, one of which likes to pull. Additionally, you can go and find specific gear recommendations to help you have a successful trip. This should be an essential guide you can keep and consult before all of your runs to have the best experience possible!

Who Am I?

My name is Bryan Barrera, and if you haven't guessed by now, I am a professional dog runner! I've been running with dogs for seven years now and turned my side hustle into one of the best dog-running companies in the country. But it helps to go back to the beginning. It should be noted that I only started running in May of 2012. I signed up for the Katy Trail 5K after a fantastic sales pitch from one of the speech pathologists who worked with me at a hospital in Dallas. Calling this thing a 5K does not do it justice; that's like calling a fancy motorcycle a bike. Yes, by definition, it is accurate, but it hardly tells the whole story. It's more like a party you run to that happens to be 3.1 miles away. With the entry fee came samples of food from forty to fifty of the best places to eat in town, free beer and margaritas, and the excellent timing of being run on a Thursday evening in near perfect (slightly warm) weather. I was bamboozled. This was my first 5K ever; I didn't learn until later how atypical this setup was. I have since become accustomed to the 8:00 a.m. Saturday starts and the bananas and bagels most races offer! Fine fare for a short run to be sure, but hardly the Cadillac expectations set by the Friends of the Katy Trail in Dallas. After that, I was bit by the running bug and continued to run faster and farther as the weeks went on. I loved the mental and physical challenge and the focus and commitment to training. Running was becoming an integral part of my life.

I once heard a local radio host say that the marathon is the most physically demanding feat of endurance that the common person can do. We don't all have the funds to travel to and climb Mount Everest, and we can't all go push the body to Iron Man limits, but we can—almost—all train for and run 26.2 miles. When I heard that, I thought, why not me?

It was early January 2013 and I was one month removed from finishing the Dallas Marathon, my first. It had been lovingly known as Dallas White Rock Marathon and had ruffled a few running-community feathers with the new name and branding. That year's route was fantastic; it crossed the new, soon-to-be-iconic Margaret Hunt Hill Bridge while still running around White Rock Lake to the northeast of the city. It proved to be the final time it circled around the lake, thus the name change. I had checked off one of the more common bucket-list items, the marathon.

Back to January 2013, and now a month had passed since the marathon. I had been going for a few thirty- to forty-five-minute runs since then. In truth, I thought I had squashed that "running bug" underneath the fifty thousand to sixty thousand steps I had taken during the race. But that little critter is definitely a cockroach, because it survived! I was thumbing through a *Runner's World* magazine and they had profiled David Hill, a man who was operating his own dog-running company. A what? A fantastic service that took aim at the issues dog walking couldn't solve. There are dogs out there that need more attention and physical exertion than a walk can offer. Running isn't a substitution for walking, it is a stand-alone offering that helps solve health and behavioral issues. It was terrific, and I thought to myself, *If I could get paid to run with dogs, THAT would get me back on a running schedule.* At the time I was living in Dallas, so I searched around and found two potential companies offering a dog-running service. The first company was operated by a sole proprietor who seemed content within the borders of downtown, a tough spot for me to get to daily. The second was a more mature company and had a wider service area but wasn't hiring at the time. I was a bit discouraged because it seemed like a great way to spend time while making a little extra spending money! I couldn't put the article down. I would read and re-read it until one night in bed I whispered to my wife, "I'm going to do it; I'm going to start my own dog-running company." She was no stranger to me saying I was going to start a business, so she gave me the requisite, "OK." I think she was a bit surprised when I started researching and drafting fliers the next day.

Of course, the doubts of starting a business crept into my head as I began to think of all the risks involved. After all, it was a bit intimidating to think about the prospect of taking a stranger's family member away from their home. But I didn't let that hold me back; I was born with an optimistic disposition and had spent years in customer service positions. I knew how to connect with people and earn trust. Being competent in our ability to provide the service for the dogs is vital, but it is connecting with families and building relationships that is at the heart of our continued success and growth.

I began researching all the different dog-running services I could find online. At the time there weren't very many, usually one or two in each major city, and far fewer that specialized in running only. What I learned from that research that still holds true through today is that many companies are general dog-service companies, and they'll do their best to help you with your needs. If that is walking, running, pet sitting, boarding, or something else, they will help you take care of your dog. I think this is a fantastic business to be in and definitely needed, but when I saw the discrepancy between general dog services and compared it against a service that specialized in running, I saw an opportunity to differentiate. I knew I wanted to spend time doing the thing that I absolutely loved—running with dogs. So right then and there I made a decision to commit to starting a company that saw running as the solution to health and behavior problems including anxiety, hyperactivity, obesity, and many others.

I was consuming everything I could on the topic, from magazine articles to blog posts to YouTube videos, and then I thought, *What if I just called David?* So, I did. I picked up the phone and cold-called him. I left a message saying I wanted to start a dog-running company in Dallas and asked if he could spend some time on a call with me. He agreed and was a wealth of knowledge. Honestly, that one-hour phone call saved me from more poking and prodding around the internet in search of answers. I found him most helpful in talking about starting and operating a dog-running company, learning the limits of the pups, and if he actually enjoyed doing it day in and day out. David was generous with his time and knowledge, and I am and will be forever thankful.

The more we talked, the more confidence I gained in being the person who could operate this kind of business. On the operations side, I had always had a quiet confidence when interacting with animals. I have never lost sight of the appropriate roles in the relationship with them, namely with them occupying a subordinate position. What I knew from experience and more research was that being dominant isn't about being tough or demonstrative or strict, but rather it is about being confident in decision-making and swift in action when the behavior falls outside expectation. Easy enough, right?

Generally, dogs are on alert and will remain so until they are confident that you are someone who can lead them. It is not always an easy transition to gain the trust of your alpha dog, but over time you can gain it. You have to spend time with them and lead the run, being patient to let them see that they are on the run with you and you are dictating the pace and distance. Making good decisions to avoid uncomfortable situations and remaining calm and confident will help you. Once you have their trust, you must respect it and keep them honest by correcting them.

On the business side, I spent enough time in sales positions with prospecting (finding customers) as a function of the job that I had a good sense of what was required to generate potential customers: social collisions. Plainly speaking, I needed to have as many interactions with dog people as I could to tell them about my wonderful (in theory) service. To stay around for as long as we have, it takes a commitment to both sides of this coin. Having a phenomenal service that nobody knows about is the same as having a poor service that has a bad reputation. No one wants to sign up for your service!

Knowing all of this, there was nothing left to do but open for business. Using Microsoft Word, I created this simple flyer (pictured below). It was me holding my oldest son, Owen, at the aforementioned Katy Trail 5K with a few bullet points about the benefits of running with dogs.

I set out for the nearest neighborhoods, going door to door and delivering them. I posted them on any community bulletin board I could find—dog shops, sandwich shops, and parks. You name it, I put a flyer on it. I created a Craigslist ad that was a direct copy and paste of the physical flyer, and then it happened … my first potential client responded by email. Could I run her eight-year-old Boykin Spaniel named Diesel? *Yes!*

The first flyer I made to start my business.

YOU DO WHAT?

Sitting here, years later, when a lot of the customer interaction comes naturally, it is easy to forget the ball of nerves and knots in my stomach as I sat there trying to convince someone to trust me with their family. After twenty minutes or so, Diesel and I set off on our "Meet & Greet." This tester run that we still do to this day gives us a chance to assess the dog's fitness and temperament as well as how well the runner and dog respond to each other.

With that first family under our belt, we leaned heavily on social media and our offline network. I set modest goals for myself and asked every friend with a dog if I could take them out running (for free). I needed to gain experience and confidence in running with one dog at a time. (I wish this book had been around at the time!) Slowly I began appearing at dog-friendly events to pass out fliers, setting up near community breakfasts at large apartment and condo buildings. Craigslist turned out to be a very good lead generator at the time, and I honed down exactly what benefits were appealing to families and what issues they were trying to solve for. Generally, families were looking for a way to expend their dog's energy, if one existed.

I learned to position the service as a way to add exercise a few days a week as opposed to an outright substitution for a week of walks. We leaned into what we did well, which was being flexible. If your dog walker came at noon, we would be there by 9 a.m. or after 3 p.m. If they came in the morning, we set up service in the afternoon or evening. Even if they wanted to replace the walk, we found a way to make it to them in the middle of the day. It was a logistical challenge, but it was the best way to get our foot in the door. I believed that once the families saw the results of running, they would sign up for more runs, and I was right! I sat in more and more homes and signed up more dogs. But, the thing that generated the most customers was word of mouth. If you are delivering value, people will notice and appreciate it and tell someone. I was an honest, dependable person who set expectations with families and their dogs and then delivered.

I started with very little knowledge about running with dogs, but I truly believe that anyone can run with their dog. What you need is a little confidence and the right information from someone who has learned on the job and made the mistakes for you! Being dedicated to the specific solution of running with your dog has not been easy, and we've seen other companies come and go. I've seen at least eight other companies outright copy our website. I suppose that's one way to get the information out! The truth is, when I see an opportunity too good to pass up, I pursue it relentlessly. When we moved to DC, we were a one-car family and couldn't afford a second, so I borrowed a bike from my brother-in-law (thanks, Vytas) and rode it to appointments. When the appointments were too far to ride to and make on time, I would ride that bike to a metro station and connect to all parts of The District. I saw the opportunity to bring a wonderful service to families who desperately needed a solution for their aggressive, anxious, and/or destructive dogs, and I helped.

You Did This by Yourself?

Absolutely not.

My wife, Suzanne, and I met while attending the University of Dallas. She is originally from the Washington, DC, area, and we agreed we would eventually make our home there. While we were still in Dallas and Dallas Dog Runner was growing, we decided the time to move was now. We had two young sons (and eventually four more children!) and knew that with every passing day it would become harder to make the move. I continued to operate the company but decided not to take on any new customers. I was solving the problems that inevitably arise from an operation, and more importantly, proved that there was a need for the service. People were so happy with the results and how their dogs behaved on days they had their runs, they almost always added additional days throughout the week. We were a valuable service that brought peace and happiness to their home. Knowing we would eventually move, I began saving every dollar Dallas Dog Runner was making. I realized there was a real opportunity to operate a side business, and with the increased living cost from Texas to the East Coast, it made sense to start researching businesses in the Washington, DC, area.

What I found was a scattering of operations that included dog running as a service under their umbrella, but none had specialized in it. I figured there was a niche to be filled. I immediately purchased the domain name and website and used the profits by re-investing in a professional logo and infographic-style flyer. I spent two months building our first website. I asked a close friend who was a busy wedding photographer if he would give action shots a try. I began stitching together the backbone of what would become DC Dog Runner.

We met for a photo shoot, and I invited every dog we were running with at the time to Highland Park, Texas. It's a beautiful town in the heart of Dallas with lush lawns, wide walkways, and manicured shrubbery. Only two people—both friends—showed up for the shoot, and I was panicked! Luckily, I'm pretty bold, so when I saw a woman with a black Labrador walking on the opposite side of the street, I walked hurriedly and explained our pickle. She just asked that I not steal her dog, a fair request. To this day, those four dogs have been mainstays on the DC Dog Runner website. I am thankful to those few in the beginning—Nick, Mia, Krysta, and random Labrador lady who helped our website make a mark by standing out with beautiful dogs and photography.

Bryan running in Highland Park, Texas.

Photo by Nick Wignall

After operating Dallas Dog Runner for about six months, we finally moved. I began drumming up business, walking streets, and flyering doors. I had already launched this exact business and knew what activity was the most beneficial. I had also been paying attention to the clients that used our service and the reasons they were looking to run, and began appealing to that. In short, I hacked my way to a launch. I would sit in living rooms, go on introductory runs and talk about the benefits of running, and repeat. Things in Washington, DC, moved much more quickly because the culture of dog walking was already healthy, so the transition to a runner from a walker for their dog was much easier. I was competing with dog walkers and not the large Texas back yards.

Often there is a moment when something seemingly out of your control happens in your business that validates and gives momentum to the idea. If you are fortunate, you can notice and appreciate it happening in real time. I wasn't so lucky, but looking back, the moment is clear, and this is it:

I had made a habit of driving the car with the windows down. When I would hear a dog barking or see one playing, I would make a note on my phone of the address and come back and flyer the whole block. On the flyer of the specific home where the dogs were, I would write a personalized note on the back introducing ourselves and signing it. Not wanting to be intrusive or run afoul of laws, we avoided knocking on doors or placing things in mailboxes. I decided the best course of action was to roll up the flyer and simply leave them wedged in door handles.

On this particular day, I was pushing my son Phillip in a running stroller to homes we would be targeting with flyers. I approached a lovely home in a charming town that abuts The District. On the face of the home there were two doors. I elected the side door in front of the driveway. I figured they used the door more often as it was glass paned and a bit more informal. When I walked up to deliver the flyer, I could see in the home, and I locked eyes with the homeowner. A shot of energy rushed through my body and, again,

I panicked—this is a common theme. A fraction of a second passed in what seemed an hour's time. He rose from his comfortable couch and greeted me at the door, and I pitched him.

"Hi, I'm Bryan, and this is Phillip! We're flyering the neighborhood and introducing ourselves to families in the area with dogs. We operate a dog-running business for active dogs who need more than a walk."

"Oh, thanks," he said. "We're actually runners, but nice to meet you."

"Have a great weekend!"

I walked away still a bit juiced from the interaction and was between their home and their neighbors when …

"WAIT!"

I was a bit startled, and my eyes darted around to see who was calling. That's when this energetic woman (Annabel) came bounding around the SUVs in the driveway. She and her husband, Matt, were both marathoners, but were also busy professionals. Their children were old enough to walk the dogs but not quite strong enough to run them.

"Wait!" she repeated.

"Hi," I said.

"Is this what you do? You run with dogs?"

"Yes."

We talked for another minute or so, and as she peppered me with questions, the enthusiasm in her voice grew.

"So, how do we start?"

That was it; that was the moment the momentum started to build. Matt and Annabel were not the first family to contract DC Dog Runner to run their dogs, but our relationship with them accounts for about one-fifth of the families we run today! The day after they started running, I received a call from their next-door neighbors Jon and Diane. Those two families, who still run with us today, are the longest-standing customers our company has. I refer to them as the "OG Crew."

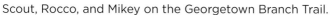

Scout, Rocco, and Mikey on the Georgetown Branch Trail.

Back to present day, DC Dog Runner is now a sixteen-person operation run by my wife and me, sharing the responsibilities we naturally gravitate toward. The easiest way to describe our setup is me as the head, whereas she is the neck. The head does nothing but sit there motionless without a functional neck. And while I am technically the sole owner of the company, it wasn't until I begged for eighteen months straight for her to join the business that she finally relented and helped give order and structure through well-thought-out processes she implemented. We've grown from a good-hearted, small, one-guy-running-with-dogs outfit to a do-it-right-or-make-it-right company that values relationships over transactions. One of the first conversations we have with new potential families is about being a human company: at some point it is likely that we are going to let them down, but our promise to them is that we are going to make it right. We've grown incredible relationships with the families we run with and are happy to have the opportunity to help *you*. Maybe we can't run with your dog, but we can help you run with them or help you find a great person to fill in and become your dog's second favorite human! Running can be a fantastic solution, and the hope is this is going to be a terrific resource to refer to as the variables to your runs with your dog change. Remember, any dog can run, but it is our job to learn how far, how fast, and how we can modify the activity to work for them and their runner.

Gwynne and Oskar running near the United States Capitol.

Photo by Chris Roden

CHAPTER TWO:
Assessing Your Dog for the First Time

Before running, the first thing to do is to gather information about your dog, and this book is a fantastic place to start. The AKC's (American Kennel Club) website for your dog is also going to give you a good base of knowledge as well as exercise recommendations. In many cases there are breed-specific clubs that can offer incredible insights into the history, jobs, and energy levels for your dog. If you know the breed of your dog, there are great resources to help you learn about their capabilities, their preferences, and styles of activity that can help you determine what kind of running may be best suited for you and your dog! If you own a rescue, there may be a little more work involved in finding the best fit. But rescue dogs are similar enough that it doesn't necessitate a wildly different approach, it just may take a little more educated guessing—as well as trial and error—to make the most impact. Some of the best runners on our roster are mixed-breed rescue dogs. We've all heard the saying, "It's not the size of the dog in the fight, but the size of the fight in the dog." That could easily be adapted and used for running. We talk a lot about fit and making sure you and your dog are the right running fit for each other.

Regardless of the dog, be it rescued or purebred, we always begin with an assessment. We can learn a lot about their temperament and fitness from a short run. Continuing to learn about your dog specifically, and what you can about their breed more generally, will be of great service to you both. Understanding your dog's temperament, ability, and desire to run are all important factors in running successfully. The great news about all of this is that you are taking an interest in your dog's physical and mental health! On the other hand, even though I'm not a fan of fear-mongering, I do like to inform families of the potential risk of long-distance running. That is such a vague term, so let's agree to define "long distance" as anything three miles—thirty minutes—and above.

When introducing physical exercise, we are looking to establish a baseline for your dog's overall health and wellness. For this I would recommend visiting with a veterinarian to inform them you would like your dog to get into a regular running routine. You should work with your veterinarian for an overall health assessment in order to hopefully receive the green light. (Later in the book I'll provide a framework of when dogs should absolutely not run and when modifications will be appropriate.) When you do speak with your veterinarian, it will be helpful for them if you can be clear with your expectations/goals. Let them know the goal is to work your dog up to three miles, three times per week. It is especially important to leave a day of rest between runs if you are just introducing long-distance running. Remember, this is just a starting point for the typical dog who goes for daily walks and the occasional dog park visit.

Now is the time to start thinking about what successful running looks like for you and your dog. Depending on your goals, below are some questions you might consider asking yourself:

- Is there a certain number of times a week you would like to get out?
- Is there a distance you would like them to run?

- Are you a runner who is trying to train them to keep up with you?
- Are you hoping to get back into running and have a dog that is ready to go but you want to do it safely?

Running with Seamus in Highland Park, Texas.
Photo by Nick Wignall

The more clearly you can define what your goals are, the better you can use this book as a guide or map to reaching that successful endpoint. Honestly, any reason that gets you out the door to spend quality time with your dog is great.

Evaluating what type of runner you are is an equally important factor that can get lost. There are a few factors to keep in mind. Obviously, knowing your fitness level and goals for yourself is important, but equally important is evaluating your temperament and how that lines up with your dog's.

No matter the dog's temperament, they are likely to respond well to a calm, confident leader. It may take some work on your end but presenting that to your dog is key and can help you enjoy your runs. Being honest and self-aware here may be tough; if you are timid and small, your dog may kick his protective instincts into overdrive. He sees you as someone he needs to be alert for. It is your job to communicate (through words and actions) that you are calm, confident, and in control.

I hold no certifications in dog training, but after spending seven years daily with hundreds of dogs, you start picking up some things. I'm naturally disposed to being aware of my surroundings at all times and was trained during my days studying biology in college to observe nature around me. With both of those tools, one gifted and the other learned, I can usually avoid hazardous situations (e.g., knowing exactly which dog I need to attend to first—to keep the pack in order—when an off-leash dog comes bounding up to my leashed pack). It's equally part instinct and part repetition that keeps me sharp and successful. Short of interacting with hundreds of dogs to learn sweeping generalities about them, you have the ability to learn the specific tendencies and situations likely to irritate your dog. Odds are you know exactly what sets your dog off! Do your best to be on alert and avoid those specific situations. For example, if you know your dog doesn't like smaller dogs, do yourself a favor and pull your dog over or walk in another direction. You can never predict how the owner of another dog you are going to cross paths with will handle a situation, so rather than let that person dictate the interaction, be proactive and be your dog's advocate by taking the proper steps to ensure a positive outcome. You can control your behavior 100 percent of the time! How many times have we heard, "Oh, he's nice!" while the dog looks as if he's two seconds from snapping the leash? That person may be right and may have let you know, but guess who doesn't know? Your dog. All he sees is a maniac dog looking to get at him or you, and his alert sensors are screaming DANGER!

A good bit of information to keep in mind is that dogs are on alert, and that alertness can manifest in a number of different behaviors. The one that can cause you grief as a runner is if it presents as defensive (protecting you/his territory) or aggressive. Your primary goal is to have confidence and maintain situational awareness. Putting your dog in successful situations is key. If the dog park isn't good for you, find a new way to socialize that keeps him near you and on a leash. Ultimately, patience and soft/slow introduction to the offending stimuli with repeated interaction will offer successful results and gain the trust of your dog.

Said another way, your dog is going to remain on alert until he trusts you have the situation under control. This has as much to do with ego as it has to do with confidence. Take the feedback your dog is giving you and find ways to do more of the things that keep him/her calm. Running is a fantastic outlet for these dogs because it focuses their attention on a task. To this day I have dogs that have run for years and are still neurotic or unfocused during the warmup walk. Then, like a switch being flipped, the anxiety, aggression, etc., melts away when we begin to run. You have given them a purpose/ job.

It is always a great idea to pool information from as many trusted sources as possible. I firmly believe that since no two dogs are the same, no two solutions are the same either, and getting all the opinions you can will help cut through the mountain of information available. A valuable resource in the ecosystem is the veterinarian. Ideally they have a file on your dog with medical history and can help you with suggestions that are tailored specifically to your dog, and in a lot of ways reinforce the information I present, or let you know that finding an alternative may be the best solution for you. I believe in dog running passionately, but I also understand that the type of running our company offers may not be the best solution for everyone. The good news is you don't necessarily have to do the type of running our company offers! You are trying to find the best fit for you and your dog, and I am here to assist. We believe in honest evaluations, and that begins with the assessment.

Assessment is such a vague word, so for our purpose, I break it down into three parts.

Assessing You as the Primary Runner—or the Person That Will Be Running the Dog

Do you want to run with your dog? I know this may seem like a ridiculous question this far into the book, but it is a valid question that will serve you and your dog best if you can give an honest evaluation of your ability. I mean this in the physical sense of keeping up on a run, but also, do you have the time to consistently devote to your dog to build a habit of running? This is not meant as a critique on lifestyle or your relationship with your dog, but are you the best fit to run with him/her?

Physical

Are you already living an active lifestyle that includes running or have an exercise regimen that is compatible? If so, you'll be able to easily adapt your current routine and devote to running with your dog three times a week. This may even require you slowing down to find a pace that works for both dog and runner. You could also find you have a training partner that will boost those race times; who knows? Are you hoping to have your active dog help you get out and run more often? If so, it is helpful to know what limits you have and how to avoid putting yourself in a hazardous situation. Are you a smaller runner who owns a big dog? This isn't impossible, but it is a factor to keep in mind. Depending on the dog's temperament and strength, you could run the pace they need but still be a bad fit. All it takes is one surprise squirrel that you don't see near a trail and the leash could yank you to the ground! An honest evaluation of your physical fitness and capabilities as compared against your dog's will yield the best results. Finding the right fit is the most important thing.

We have a runner who is fantastic at all parts of the job. Honest, friendly, timely, and dedicated. The superlatives go on glowingly. As fantastic as she is at almost every aspect of the job with one dog, the dynamics changed anytime she ran with two dogs at the same time. Even if the dogs were friendly and mostly relaxed and got along, problems arose. There was a dust-up between two dogs from the same home; this was unusual because when I ran with them, they were well behaved. Incidents happen, and we address them and move forward. A second and unrelated incident happened that required us to sit down and discuss solutions.

It turns out that our runner who was game to run with multiple dogs had a bit of underlying hesitance; these dogs sensed it almost immediately and threw off the dynamic of the entire pack and left things feeling unsettled. With an honest self-evaluation, we agreed that her best fit was with one dog at a time. From an efficiency and business standpoint, not ideal, but from a safety and comfort perspective, going to a solo dog run made the most sense.

A big key in our culture and decision-making is to always value the relationship over the transaction. Putting our runners and our families' dogs in the best and safest running situation is always going to win the day.

Temperament

In my opinion, this evaluation is one of the most important for this entire relationship to work. Understanding your disposition and how that is related to your dog is vital. Think of the leash as a direct line between your attitude and energy and your dog's. They'll pick up on your tension (if present), and they'll be on high alert. It's likely you have good reason to have the feelings, but knowing that they affect your dog's behavior is important, too. I'm not asking you to change your natural intuition, in fact, just the opposite. I think your instincts probably serve you well, but if they don't mesh well with your dog's temperament, you need to know it. In my experience, when evaluating potential runners, characteristics I value are quiet, calm, and confidence as it pertains to redirecting the dog's attention. Heavy-handed disciplinarians and soft-loving (positive reinforcement) advocates definitely have their successful outcomes, but being a steady, calm, and confident pack leader that doesn't easily fluster when confronted by an unruly dog will serve you best. Dogs are always going to be dogs, and how they respond is unique and hard-wired into who they are. We cannot control that, but we can control how we govern it and what we do to bring the situation back to neutral. Knowing your inclination as it relates to your dog's will help you in the long run.

Assessing Your Dog

Physical Fitness

Much like their human running counterparts, it can take time to build stamina, and being conservative with mileage is only going to help with the long-term goal of building the habit of running. This part of the assessment is your chance to look at the overall activity of your dog. Are they already a fantastic runner and you need a little extra help? Are you trying to get them to lose a few pounds because you've been a little too loving with the treats?

1. Is your dog a sprinter?
2. Is your dog overweight?
3. Are they a puppy or an older dog?
4. Do they have any pre-existing conditions like hip dysplasia you will need to monitor?

Learning all of this valuable information on the front end of the process will help you set realistic expectations and give you a starting point that works well for both dog and runner.

Harper, Heidi, Bear, Maximus, Scout, and Beckett in Georgetown.

After calling your veterinarian to discuss running and health, the first thing you should do is go on a fartlek! A funny word for sure, but also a fantastic exercise, it's Swedish for "speed play." It is a combination of running, walking, and sprinting, repeated in no particular order and for no specified distance or duration for each cycle or individual exercise. I recommend aiming for a twelve- to twenty-five-minute outing on your first go-round. Rely on your instincts. For instance, walk to the end of the block from your door, sprint to the next stop sign you see, then jog to the sixth light pole. Just pick highly visible endpoints like trees, homes, and intersections to determine the change in activity; you should always know your end-point before beginning. Keep in mind that you should be monitoring your dog's energy level as well as level of interest in the activity. Most dogs will be super excited, but the first off-ramp to running would be their hesitance to run or sprint. You should always be watching and evaluating.

Gathering all of this information will tell you what type of running your dog likes. Chances are, if you've picked up this book, you're thinking about those nice long thirty-plus-minute runs with your dog, but with an honest evaluation, you may be able to determine that short sprints are more appropriate for your dog. In all cases, tailor your workouts to maximize your dog's happy zone. If they like to pace right next to you for an hour, enjoy it! If they like to go full tilt and then rest, work that into the mix. More important than willing your dog to an activity you prefer, it's best if you find the right fit for them.

Temperament

In the same way that you know your own responses and reactions, you have probably learned how your dog responds, too. The questions I like to find the answers to are:

1. Any aggression toward people?
2. Any aggression toward other dogs?
3. Is it localized (one dog on the block) or general (e.g., smaller dogs)?
4. What is their response to loud noises—trucks, buses, fire engines, sirens, etc.?
5. How do they respond to skateboards, scooters, cyclists? Do they even notice? Do they lunge or bark?
6. Do they like to pull, or do they prefer a side to run on?
7. Do they veer or run straight?
8. Do they like to run by your side or be given their own space?

The idea is to get a general sense of what your dog(s) prefers and how they respond to external stimuli. The best evaluation is an honest one, and for long-term success, it takes the self-awareness that you may not be the best fit or that the goal needs to be modified. Nothing is ironclad, and in truth, you should make a habit out of evaluating and re-evaluating with each new season: (1) for the changes in external factors, but also (2) for the changes in your strength and stamina, and the same for your dog.

Age

Additional information to consider is the age of your dog when you begin running. I'll reiterate this again in later chapters, but running with puppies twelve months or younger (and in some breeds up to fifteen months) can lead to lasting injuries if the puppy isn't developed enough.

Exercising patience is key during the first months with a puppy. The toughest conversations I consistently have are with owners of puppies fifteen months and younger. In conflict is the insatiable need for attention and energy of a puppy against safe growth and development of their physical health. Make no mistake, the puppy energy is real. They will test patience and nerves with their incessant need for attention and activity. The best solution is to make sure they are tired while also ensuring that you are doing so safely. In these formative months they are growing rapidly and consistent long-distance running could lead to stress on the growth plates, bones, and ligaments. Running is not a bad activity, but running long distances on consecutive days could expose your young dog to avoidable long-lasting injuries. Hip dysplasia is a developmental issue in the hip joint where the ball at the top of the leg doesn't fit with the socket in the hip. I know the investment in time and dollars in young pups can stretch the limits of reason and sanity. I'm convinced that this is why they are so cute. If they weren't, their "pain in the butt" quotient would have limited their popularity as loved family members!

We use fifteen months to be conservative, but put the absolute no long-distance running on any puppy younger than twelve months. Likewise, we need to take special precautions when assessing our overweight and elder dog population. Easing into the activities with plenty of rest days built in will help maintain and build physical and cardiovascular strength. Adjust expectations of these types of runners and factor in that they may need more walk breaks and slower paces. Keep an eye on any hitches or hobbling in their gait. Always back off and adjust the activity or allow the proper time to rest. Sometimes getting those old bones, joints, and muscles activated adds stress on the dog, even if the desire is present. If the injury lingers, consult your vet.

The assessment is an important step in getting out running successfully, so be attentive and take your time. Remember that assessing your dog is only half of the equation, and assessing yourself honestly will benefit you both greatly! I have no doubt that the notes provided here will give you great information that will help you determine the type of runner your dog is, goals you can set, and finally, if you are the best fit for running with your dog. Running with your dog can be fun for both of you if you set the right expectation.

Types of Dogs

The Sprinter

These dogs are not built for and do not love the long-distance run, but they like to give it their all for short bursts, catch their breath, and then do it all over again. Generally speaking, they have compact torsos with muscular builds. If they love going to the dog park and play chase or fetching the ball for an hour, they're likely a sprinter. If they bounce all over the place, are continuously out front, and you feel like you are having to hold them back, they are a sprinter. These dogs have a real sense of joy about them when they run, which is why they probably just want to get after it. The sprinter lends itself to a runner that can give them one-on-one attention to harness (no pun intended) that energy and control the pace to run longer or a runner that can adapt to include more sprinting and resting!

The Road Warrior

A steady companion that will run near you on a leash and chew up the asphalt and dirt trail miles alike. This is, generally speaking, the type of dog I spend my time with because: (1) it is our policy to remain on a leash due to the strict leash laws, and (2) our services are the best fit for this type of runner—even if they prefer another style, this way they can run with packs.

The Trail Dog

Some dogs insist on running off-leash and in nature. They are predisposed to be a little more free and have the proper training and call-back (returning to their owner when called) to warrant such

Bryan with Limmy, Penny, Tahoe, and Cappy running through Cabin John Park in Potomac, Maryland.

trust. Remember to always obey leash laws in your area, and if it is an option for you, get out on the open trails! There are a few things I recommend before unleashing in the wild:

- Proper off-leash training: Make sure you can trust your dog not to be a nuisance to others enjoying the trail. Expect to assume responsibility if they come across a leashed dog and fireworks happen. Even though you know your dog well, you can't possibly know the temperament and relationship with any dogs (or other animals) he comes across when you are out of sight.

- Ensure that your dog is properly chipped, and consider investing in an external GPS device attached to their collar or vest.

- Invest in a brightly colored vest (yellow/orange) for your dog when off-leash. This will help you keep an eye out if they veer off the trail and into thicker forested areas, and help other trail users, runners, and bikers be able to tell what type of animal is near.

Sarah and Millie running in Georgetown.

Photo by Chris Roden

CHAPTER THREE:
Reasons for Running With Your Dog

There are so many reasons to begin and continue running with your dog. It obviously provides them with physical stimulation that most dogs just aren't getting, but it also provides mental stimulation. Remember that dogs were originally asked to help get work done, meaning they had a job or purpose, whether it was the Border Collie helping the farmer herd sheep, or Dalmatians running out in front of the fire truck to alert the community what was coming behind. Even beyond that, some were trained to protect our homes and businesses. Over time, dogs have become more family than workforce, although some still provide valuable assistance to the blind, or as part of military and police forces. Like us, dogs want to feel safe and secure, and when they don't it can present in many ways.

In this section of the book, I'll take a look at some of the more common reasons for running with your dog, and how it can help. But in order to better understand these reasons, we need to think about the evolution and purpose of dogs in our lives and how it has changed in the last forty years. Once dogs were only seen as working aids; they helped in protection and many other jobs. Shepherds and collies

Henry and Lisa running in Old Town Alexandria, Virginia.

Photo by Chris Roden

helped ranchers; Portuguese waterdogs helped fishermen; Dalmatians were known to protect firemen, and German shepherds helped police and military. In years past, domestic dogs were typically property of the wealthy. I can't imagine there were too many dog owners during the Great Depression; taking on the additional cost of a pet without the benefit of helping probably wasn't a high priority.

Many things have contributed to our present relationship with dogs and their lifestyle. The attitudes toward dogs being seen as family members have risen dramatically, and shelter adoption rates echo this thought. A predominantly work-based relationship and dynamic gave way to domestication and companionship. But the trend toward responsible dog ownership is trending up. In some instances, dogs are still asked to help with work, but by and large, they are considered members of the family. What they were bred to do and how they live today are in conflict. They live mostly sedentary lives with daily walks, occasional play, and hearty meals. Long gone are the days of earning your keep and burning calories in the fields and farms. But enough about what caused the problem. How do we fix it?

I've found it helpful to group the reasons people commonly want to run with their dog into two categories: health and behavioral. That seems like a natural division of the spectrum that sets physical needs on one side and mental on the other. It is also common that some combination of health and behavior leads to owners searching for a solution.

We'll break down these reasons and how running helps you and your dog. Running is not the only solution, but it can greatly assist in whatever changes, either fitness or behavioral, you are looking to affect.

Health

Reduce Fat and Obesity

Maybe you have not been proactive, and your veterinarian suggested a goal of losing weight because your dog is overweight or even obese! This is not uncommon, unfortunately, as an estimated 56 percent of dogs in the United States are overweight and obese. Can we be surprised when we see statistics as eye-popping as that? Rather than dwelling on the decisions and missteps that led us here, let's begin the conversation about how to correct it!

Being realistic and conservative about the approach will greatly assist in finding a lasting solution. The weight wasn't gained over a day, weekend, or month, and you shouldn't set an aggressive plan to try and course-correct overnight. Dogs are similar to us in that they will benefit from a little ramp up to activity. Start by introducing a trot a couple of times a week using some light intermittent jogging.

Do not worry about introducing exercise on a leash yet, just work on getting the heart rate up and blood pumping. Chase them around and let them chase you. Commit to and incorporate spending time in ways they already like to be active. Throw all the balls, and if they like running at the dog park, make a concerted effort to take them one to two more times per week. All of this is preventative, and work needs to be done before introducing running. Keep it fun! In tandem, follow the dietary guidelines your veterinarian recommends. Once physical activity is more a part of their routine and lifestyle, use this guide to introduce and increase workload while running. Do it with intention and purpose, pay attention to the feedback, and modify appropriately. If they are laboring to breathe, or you have a taut leash because they are dragging behind, slow the pace or take a

Gwynne and Oskar running down East Capitol Street in NE Washington, DC.

Photo by Chris Roden

break. Use your instincts to pull back when you think your dog is no longer enjoying the exercise.

Build Muscle

Like any form of physical activity, the results are dependent on the effort put in. Using running as a means to build muscle requires an intentional approach. Once the pounds have started to melt away, you can specialize and tailor the workouts to show growth in areas you want. To begin building muscle, incorporate shorter sprints into your long-distance running routine. An old running adage is that hills are speedwork in disguise. Start at the bottom of the hill and run up, or throw the ball from the bottom of the hill up! Be cautious with these exercises, and as always, introduce them slowly.

Nicole with Rocco, Wookie, Mikey, and Scout.

Photo by Chris Roden

Some would ask about the need or benefit of building muscle. First, it helps relieve stress from joints and ligaments long term, and for those dogs that have matured, it can help as they approach elder years and muscle mass begins to diminish. As with humans who are leaving their prime, keeping muscles from atrophy needs to be a deliberate and conscious decision, and beginning the habits to counteract it later (nine+ years old) begins during the years they still have muscle and strength!

Another way to use running to build muscle is to incorporate running with weighted vests. Vests can be filled with sandbags for running around town or more functionally to cart around your supplies on longer trail runs. The additional weight only adds to the sense of work and purpose for the dogs. As your dog builds strength and muscle, you can maintain or increase capacity.

Behavioral Reasons

Anxiety

This is characterized by a nervousness or inability to remain calm when exposed to seemingly normal everyday stimuli. These dogs will remain on high alert in both new and familiar situations. Anxiety is a common reason that a family will contact our service to run with their dog. We like to do a little fact-finding during phone conversations with families to determine what is causing the anxiety. During the interview with the families we do our best uncover any issues they think running could help with. This is before I meet the dog so that I can have a good frame of reference and approach the introduction appropriately. Is the anxiety caused by the family? In a lot of ways, the anxiety of the family can add stress to the existence of their dog. Sometimes the family knows they are part of the cause of anxiety and other times they do not. What they do share, though, is a desire to be part of the solution. They've heard running may offer them a little assistance. It's possible that the anxiety has led to a recoiling from social activities, that their dog has become a source of pain and trepidation. I've known one of the members of the family to stop taking their dog out altogether because of the anxiety. Do not let fear take the joy out of your relationship with your dog.

- **Bad Interactions:** I've heard the story dozens of times that a family's dog was the happy-go-lucky type that ran into a rambunctious dog who didn't play nice or took a specific malicious interest in their dog. These things happen, and they are no one's fault. Sometimes dogs (like people) just aren't meant to get along. It doesn't mean they are bad dogs, it just means that they need to be put in situations to succeed, and that goes for both the aggressor and the attacked. There are some times when a dog gives off some sort of signal that other dogs pick up on, and they become the dog that attracts negative attention.
- **Weather:** Sometimes dogs have a hard time in inclement weather. They are sensitive to rain or snow and do not like getting wet or cold. But most often it is the weather paired with lightning and thunder that can cause the most anxiety. If affected, dogs will cower or shake when they hear and feel the percussion and can become like statues and refuse to move. Even at home and not on the run, you'll see evidence of the fear. A thunder shirt is a good solution to help this anxiety. It is a specialty compression shirt that can be worn around the home. I would advise against them being used during runs because of the restriction, but the likelihood is that you are not going out into the storm but instead have found yourself caught by one.
- **Loud noises:** Similar to the percussion of thunder, fireworks cause a lot of unrest for dogs. You may have noticed the warning signs or posts on social media about keeping your dog inside during the 4th of July celebrations. These sounds can strike terror in dogs (dogs have been known to panic and escape an enclosure trying to get away). For those of you that are in the city, it is common for us to ask about their response to buses, dump trucks, fire

trucks, and motorcycles. They are usually less frequently reactive to these, but the response can be similar or can be more aggressive with dogs lunging or barking at them as they pass.

- **Men:** It is not uncommon for dogs to be reactive to men, and sometimes it is specifically men with hats. Fair or not, understanding that this is the case, you can do your best to maintain a safe distance for you, your dog's mental state, and the physical safety of men. I don't know the reason, but I do know that I have made a note of it after dozens of "meet and greets" with prospective families. This can manifest as either passive (cowering/moving away) or more likely aggressive (barking/showing teeth) while their fur stands up and they want to lunge. When introducing someone new to your dog, it is a good idea to have them keep their distance and remain patient. Have both the person and dog stay in the room, or even bringing the dog out of the home but staying in their presence is key. Take your time with this so they begin to see them as part of the environment as opposed to an intruder encroaching on their space. As time passes you can walk together with them and close the space and eventually have them take over the leash. If the dog doesn't warm up completely, ask them to come back another day and repeat the process. Making things normal and routine will go a long way in establishing a relationship and building trust. As you will find out, I am a huge proponent for being active and maybe slightly unorthodox with solutions. My aim is to always put the dog at ease, especially in the home. You can work with a trainer to pinpoint the exact cause, but this could be a good start, especially if the person is a frequent visitor.

- **Separation Anxiety:** This happens for both dogs and people. And when your dog senses it in you, he knows something is off and responds to it. He will whine or bark and nothing seems to help. Short of you working from home, or having multiple walks throughout the day, running can help by tiring them out, giving them something to focus on, and calming

Nicole with Wookie and Rocco running on Rock Creek Trail.

Photo by Chris Roden

the excess anxiety because they are being stimulated physically and mentally. He will get the companionship and bonding he is looking for. Remember to tread carefully into these situations and take into consideration your temperament and act accordingly. My approach is calm and matter of fact, assuming nothing is upsetting and powering through hesitations. But do not be stubborn; if treats help, use them, but realize you may be unwittingly reinforcing the behavior.

We have this wonderful owner that called specifically about running as a calming solution for their dog. The dog has the athleticism, stamina, and desire to run, but has a hard time with separation anxiety. This showed up on our initial visit, and to the owner's credit, she thought it might go poorly. The dog warmed right up, coming over to sniff, wagging her tail, and generally being a wonderful host. There were no stop signs and the only concern was from the information provided by the family. When first meeting any new family, I try to take the dog with the same gear setup that they use. This can be a standard leash and collar or a harness or halter. We do this because we want to keep the first run as close to their normal routine as possible. As I assess the dog and situation, I can make recommendations on ways to improve. The dog, Millie, walked with me to the door. The family lives in a walk-up unit that has an exterior stairwell. We made it down one half-flight and, STOP! Millie applied the brakes. She became a statue; she did not pull back, she did not whine or yelp, she just stood still and refused to move. Generally, a little coaxing, treat-giving, and time are all we need to overcome some stubbornness. But after eight to ten minutes, I called it a day and moved it back up the stairs and into the home. Rather than coming back another day, I thought of other ways to solve the issue and decided to send a female runner from our company. Initially, Millie hesitated but did eventually go. Fast forward five months, and I was tasked with running Millie again. We had to find a solution or risk losing the progress Millie made. It turns out Millie didn't mind leaving her home, she didn't want to leave her human. With her owner gone, she hesitated, and still does, but the runs are successful and enjoyable.

Picking up on the Cues of Anxiety:

- Their tail is hanging low and tucked close to their body.
- The majority of their movement is backward and away from the social interaction.
- They begin to shake.
- They begin to yelp and whine as though distressed.

Lisa and Henry running in Old Town Alexandria, Virginia.
Photo by Chris Roden

- Unusual activity in their ears, pointing, standing up or back.
- Their fur will stand up around the neck and back.

Hyperactivity

Some dogs just have a hard time turning their internal motors off, and they never seem to tire or stop moving. They are on constant alert and wanting to be a part of and involved in everything. Walks do not seem to work, and going to the dog park every day is just not realistic. It is always helpful to know the history of your dog and the recommended exercise for the breed. But with that being said, some dogs are just born with rocket boosters strapped to them. They will bark at the door and jump up on guests or strangers; they just cannot seem to contain themselves. They are generally very friendly and have an eager personality. These are the kind of dogs that you'll take for an hour-long ball-throwing session only to have them doing circles around the living room coffee table and running back and forth across the house. You can let them out in the yard, but it's just never enough. Running helps to physically exhaust them by using some of that pent-up energy, but equally important is the mental stimulation and engagement offered. They will have a sense of purpose and work, and focus on the run— both in tandem should offer some relief, even if only for the evening!

Aggressiveness

Every so often we get a dog that can no longer go on pack walks or play at the local dog park because they have shown themselves to be aggressive or incapable of playing nice with a specific dog, or dogs in general. It is possible he will fight, nip, or even worse, already have bitten other dogs or people. This can sometimes mean doggy day care is off the table as a solution and walks can become difficult. Running, on the other hand, can be a fantastic solution because they have something to focus on and the opportunity for interaction can be limited. When on a dog walk there's a likelihood you come across another dog on a walk, and there is the verbal or non-verbal agreement whether you should or shouldn't introduce your dogs. However, when running, people are less likely to stop you because you have an implied purpose. Ideally, they'll pull to the side and let you on through, but people aren't always the most self-aware, so it is incumbent on you to know your dog, and if you see you are headed toward a social collision, stop and alter your course. Either off the sidewalk and into the road, off the path—stopping with enough room for them to safely pass—or turn around and run the opposite direction. If the other family is courteous, they'll quickly walk past and even offer a "Thank you!" But remember, momentarily checking your ego and thinking what you can control, your dog and body positioning specifically, can keep you out of a bad situation where a dog or person could be hurt.

Destructiveness

This is the outward expression of anxiety, hyperactivity, or even boredom marked by biting, scratching, and causing physical damage (usually while unattended) to personal belongings. The source of the frustration can vary wildly from a dog who is protesting being left alone, to boredom and giving themselves the job of defabric-ing the sofa cushion. But, it is likely just pent-up energy, and they start to work on something like the baseboards or gnawing on shoes. Obviously talking through solutions with a trainer and behaviorist is a great idea, but running can absolutely be part of the equation.

Whatever your reason for wanting to run with your dog, or have them run, you are not alone. The aim of helping stimulate them physically and mentally is all oriented toward providing happiness for your dog, for you, and in your relationship with one another. Your "Why" is the most important factor in the equation. We can help with answering the "Who" and "How." Having a goal and with our assistance, a plan of action will set you on a path to success.

Remember that it is in your dog's nature to want to work, be active, and run. It wasn't that long ago they were field hands and contributing members to the household. They are made to do more than sit around the home waiting for you!

Nicole with Rocco, Wookie, Scout, and Mikey.

Photo by Chris Roden

CHAPTER FOUR:
Tools for Running with Your Dog

To this point I've introduced myself, explored the value of assessing your dog and yourself for running, and explained the reasons our dogs need to run. Here, in chapter four, I want to dive into the gear that is going to help you on your runs. Some are non-negotiable—collars with up-to-date tags and a leash—but there are many other tools that can help you. The aim of use for any gear should be for it to empower you to take your dog out with confidence.

On every meet and greet, I do my best to strip the gear down to a minimum. If we can go out comfortably with just a standard leash and collar, I consider that to be the best-case scenario. Second to that, I will have them use their typical gear setup and leave the home, so the dog is at least familiar with the tools—if they aren't familiar with me. If the run is too much work because the dog is unable to focus or continues to pull or has bouts of difficult-to-control outbursts, aggression, or overeagerness, I will recommend specific solutions for the dog.

The most common need for added gear is caused by straight line-pulling. They want to go forward at breakneck speed! I'll share with you solutions that have worked for me, but always follow your instincts and the choices that get the best results for you. Whatever makes you feel confident and comfortable is going to translate into a positive interaction with your dog!

Tools

My thoughts on tools is that they are all designed and engineered to help assist you in comfortably moving with your dog. Our job as owners and professionals is to find the best solution for each dog. We shouldn't expect to find a specific tool be the answer for every dog. I know it probably worked for your friend and his dog, but the reality is that you, your dog, and most importantly, your relationship are different. Don't be discouraged if the tools recommended to you do not work as well for you; be prepared to invest time and resources into finding the best solution. The last thing you want to do is think about the potential headache of running with your dog because you've been using the wrong tools. Companies invest large amounts of money and have solved the issue for a segment of the population. There is a solution for you, too, so do your best to find it!

Bryan and Sarah running with Gracie, Lentil, Cleo, Harper, and Millie near the Georgetown Waterfront.

Photo by Chris Roden

Leashes

wagwear - Nylon Metropolitan Leash

Specs: 3 to 6 feet long, ¾ inch or 1 inch wide; dual end bolt snaps; 3 D-rings for length adjustment; nylon cordura

My favorite solution for running with multiple dogs is the Nylon Metropolitan Leash made by wagwear. I came across this leash when I used one that belonged to a family I run with. After one use, I searched the internet for it and promptly ordered one. The genius behind its design is the double-ended bolt snap coupled with three D-rings that allow you to choose a length between three, four, and six feet. Plus, the ability to loop another leash through one end and bolt-snap to the nearest D-ring creates a handle, thereby allowing you to comfortably and safely run with multiple dogs while only needing to hold onto one leash. (Almost all dog leashes have one bolt snap end and one handle end.) You'll find that any solution that allows you a free hand with multiple dogs is well worth the investment, and this tool measures up!

KONG® Comfort Traffic Dog Leash

Specs: 4 feet long, 1 inch wide; 2 padded handles; bolt snap; nylon

In my opinion this is a fantastic, versatile, single-dog-running tool that is great for new and experienced runners alike. It measures four feet long by one inch wide and is made of nylon. It has two handles, with the typical handle at the end of the leash, plus the additional "traffic" handle near the bolt snap end connecting to the collar or harness on the dog. This design comes in handy—pardon the pun—to maintain maximum control of the dog when pressed into action to change directions quickly. What sets the KONG® Comfort Traffic Dog Leash apart from other makers with similar designs is that both handles are padded.

This padding can save you some serious leash burn on your palms. It allows you a spot to grab that will remain static without fearing the leash being drawn across your free hand. It is best for city running, but also great for trails. Occasionally, you'll be faced with a situation that will require quick thinking and fast action—a bicycle will come whizzing past, a skateboard or scooter will not yield at an intersection, a car that didn't see you will take a turn thinking it is clear. With this tool, you'll be able to reach down to grab the secondary "traffic" handle to pull the dog nearer to you.

The goal in any of these situations is to reduce the distance between yourself and the dog with maximum control. The second handle is the key to redirecting them safely and quickly. The leash is only four feet long, so the dog is near to begin. I'd recommend running with a bend in your arm so that you have physics on your side. With that bend, the muscle is engaged, and you have a natural lever to pull the dog closer. If the arm is fully extended, it can be a bit tougher to draw the dog closer. Once the distance begins to close, you can grab the secondary handle with your free hand, giving you two points of contact and better control.

Bryan with Heidi using a KONG® Comfort Traffic Dog Leash.

If you have a dog that is reactive, on high alert, or has a tendency to lunge, learning to run two-handed can be helpful, although holding both handles simultaneously may require a little practice. With the dog running on your right, hold the end handle in your left hand and the traffic handle with your right and run with it just above your belt height with arms bent slightly. If something catches your dog's attention and he reacts, pull both hands to your hips and pivot around your away foot (in this example, the left). This will guide your dog in the direction you prefer and away from the source of excitement. When coupled with a head-halter, the results are incredible. I love this leash; it's great for everyday use. It is a fixed length, which I feel is the safest for you, runners, walkers, and other dogs around.

Bungee Leash

These leashes have mixed reviews and are a matter of taste. I personally don't like the expansion and compression and anything that affects the normal gait of running; I find it is sort of like a delayed whiplash effect. I also understand that some people recommend them as the best use for hands-free running and use them almost exclusively. Definitely a potential solution for a one dog/one runner situation, but adding multiple dogs can become cumbersome and compromise safety. Bungee leashes take a couple of different forms. Both are designed to help absorb some of the shock of a dog who likes to pull. I highly recommend walking your dog on this type of leash before heading out for the run. Knowing how the leash responds to tension is key to identifying if this is the leash for you. The idea is that the leash absorbs some of the force as your dog runs away from you. It expands its length a few inches and slows the rate of acceleration (slightly) of your dog, rather than the length remaining static and the force transferred to you and your dog completely. This results in either you being pulled off balance to the direction your dog wants to go, or stops the momentum of your dog more abruptly and back in your general direction. This becomes dangerous the longer the static length is because there is built-up slack.

When the slack runs out, the full force is transferred to you and the dog. The bungee definitely reduces this but does take a little time and experience to become comfortable with because it is an interesting sensation. You know the direction you are about to go in, it just takes a little more time for the physics to play out.

The first kind is with a segment of bungee built into an otherwise standard leash. This gives you maybe three to six inches of play. The second is where the majority, if not the entirety, of the leash is bungee-like, and the difference between the resting and activated length can be a foot or more. Think of it like curly hair, when straightened, the length can be surprising! What I have noticed is a wave-like yo-yo effect when running, where the distance between you and the dog is expanding and constricting rhythmically. If you can get the cadence and feel down and, it can be enjoyable. A lot of very fast professional Canicross athletes use them exclusively. They can be a great tool, just factor in a bit of trial by fire when learning to use them.

Megan and David with Lentil, Bear, and Maximus.
Photo by Chris Roden

Retractable Leashes

This is another tool that receives its fair share of criticism. Honestly, apart from some of the horror stories you can find online, I would just say that the bulkiness of the handle makes it an impractical tool for running with your dog. Couple that with the fact that you may find yourself running on difficult terrain or places that are unfamiliar at times, it increases the opportunity that you will experience some potential error.

Most of the issues with retractable leashes are a function of user error. You do not get accustomed to a set distance between you and the dog, and neither does he. The biggest culprit is injury caused by too much slack in the line. There is play in the retractable leash when your dog runs after something.

1. You notice, and you stop the leash, but there is slack built up so he has five extra feet to run. With that extra room, he can pull you over or put pressure on your arm from the shoulder to the wrist and fingers. A lot of opportunity for injury.

2. You notice and can't retract soon enough. They exhaust the entire leash distance and can pull you over or dislocate a shoulder. If the force is too much to hold onto, the leash will go flying from your hand, and the dog is running free with the plastic handle that can get caught on something. Not only do you risk injury to yourself, but also to your dog. If it is attached to his neck or head, your dog could sustain injuries to their neck if pulled back violently, as is possible when the leash becomes taut. I'm sure these can be fine tools for calm, well-behaved dogs who are not a flight risk, but for active dogs who are running, I would strongly discourage their use. There are better-fit leashes when the objective is running safely for you and your dog.

Couplers

This is a helpful tool that allows you to run with two dogs without needing to use two leashes. The fewer leashes you can have while still maintaining control is going to be a benefit and reduce your chances of tripping, or having a leash snag on something. This is more of a leash extension that connects one leash to two dogs. It is made of nylon with an O-ring that connects to the pieces of nylon (twelve to eighteen inches) and has bolt snaps at each end. Connect your leash to the middle O-ring and you're able to walk two dogs with only one leash. This is a fantastic solution to use when you have two well-behaved dogs. It solves the issue of dogs jockeying for position and turning and twisting multiple leashes around each other, or worse, you. The key to running safely is knowing where the dogs are. Ideally, keep them in front of you or to one side, never behind. If they are at the end of one leash, they are easier and safer to run. The drawback is that as one dog goes, so does the other, with twice the force. It may not be the best fit if one dog likes to lead and the other falls behind, because they will be at odds and you'll have to decide to speed one up or slow the other down.

Bryan with Fayde, Jade, and Seamus using a coupler.
Photo by Nick Wignall

Collars

Flat Collar

This is the standard everyday collar we see most often. Made of nylon, leather, or some other material, it lies comfortably against the neck of the dog and has a single D-ring to attach a leash. This is the most basic necessity of having a dog outside. There is a ring to attach a leash and ID tags. The designs and colors are endless and range from low to high end. Best-case scenario, this collar and a standard leash will be enough for you and your dog. You can get them in all manner of material, with padding or lined for comfort.

Martingale Collar

This collar is made of two parts (loops): The first loop is the flat collar portion that is a fixed size and meant to rest loosely around the neck of your dog. The second loop connects the ends of the first loop and can be made of nylon or steel chain. This loop is used to control the dog when the leash is attached. As the dog pulls, the collar tightens. This is a useful tool when training your dog to run if you don't like the choke collar or prong collar. It is a great fit for dogs that are escape artists or flight risks, particularly if they have smaller heads. When a dog gets scared, his instinct is to get away. Often, this means stopping and trying to back out of a collar. If a standard collar is a little loose, they can slip right out and bolt anywhere. The brilliance of the martingale is that as the dog moves back and away, the design restricts the smaller second loop so the head cannot wriggle loose. I'm a big fan of the martingale for dogs who are reactive and may have an instinct to run away when loose.

Choke Collar

This is a simple collar typically made of a steel chain connecting two O-rings, but I've also seen them made of thin cords. Generally, they are thin and can be used in tandem with other standard collars as a failsafe, so the dog doesn't escape.

Slip one part of the chain through one of the O-rings and your dog's head through that loop. Attach your leash to the free O-ring, and the collar is ready for use. Like the martingale, it is meant to be worn loosely but to tighten as tension is applied to the leash. Meaning, if your dog begins to pull, it tightens. This is best used for training and someone who can keep a vigilant eye on their dog and remain proactive.

The purpose of the choke collar is to use it to get their attention while on the move. I've had the best results letting the collar sit high on the neck, close to the jowls, and pulling up on the leash rather than back. The idea is to raise the head to make it uncomfortable rather than cutting air supply, as the name choke implies. A quick popping action with the wrist is more than enough to get their attention because it restricts then frees the head momentarily. The only time it should be restricted for longer than that moment is if the dog is pulling away from you to chase after something and you are trying to regain control. But even in this scenario, it is the dog's action causing the choking response and not the pulling on the neck.

Prong Collar

This is a metal resizable collar with independent links that can be removed or added to adjust the circumference of the collar. There are inward-facing prongs on each link that help to get the attention of the dog when they are distracted or reacting to negative stimulation. The design is identical to the martingale but with metal components for the prongs. I've also seen a plastic version of the prong collar that looks less intimidating while providing the same function. It has a smooth exterior as opposed to interlinking metal pieces. Likewise, the component that pulls taught to restrict the plastic prong portion is made of nylon cord. The key to this tool is to do your homework and learn how to properly use it. It can be intimidating, and can cause a negative reaction to dog owners who aren't familiar with it. I can see how it appears like a dangerous tool, but the fact is, when used correctly, it is very effective. I would definitely recommend this for running if your dog has random bursts of energy or a tendency to get riled up when other humans, dogs, or rodents come near.

It is designed to distribute the pressure around the neck of the dog evenly as opposed to a standard leash that can apply the pressure directly to the trachea. When a dog is running out front or pulling and is constantly being held back, your natural reaction is to slow them down by pulling them back. With proper training, this tool can help you get your dog's attention quickly and keep them from causing damage to important structures in the throat.

Both Scout and Cole in Meridian Hill Park using prong collars.

Electric Collar

To date, I have successfully avoided needing an electric collar. I think they are useful training tools when reinforcing the desired behaviors. I feel that running already requires enough of your attention and your dexterity that giving that up for the remote control isn't worth the trade-off. Similar to the retractable leash, it requires accuracy under duress to be effective, and things between dogs can develop very quickly that your reaction time and ability to safely administer the function of the collar can be tested. Like most tools, it requires proper knowledge and training on use as well as comfort with the device so that it will be an effective tool in teaching. I know some trail runners that run with their dogs off-leash that use it as a callback with low currents to let the dog know when they need to return or stay closer to their runner. There are other, better solutions for running than the electric collar in my opinion.

Harnesses

Gentle Leader

I think this delivers incredible results if the dog will accept it. Some dogs just don't have the patience to wear a harness around their head and can potentially cause irritation and wounds from scratching in effort to get it off. For dogs who have a desire to pull, but do accept the Gentle Leader, I have seen excellent results. Halti is another brand that I like because of the extra bolt snap that connects the head harness to the everyday collar and around the head. It is also thicker and more substantial by its design. It can sometimes be confused with a muzzle because it does wrap across the bridge of the nose and below the mouth near the jaw, but this does not restrict the dog's ability to breathe, drink, or bite. The idea behind this solution is that it gives you full control of their head, and if you control the head, you control the dog. By design, if they begin to pull forward it turns their head back toward you slightly to create a mild discomfort in order for them to stop pulling. Because the neck begins to turn back, it doesn't allow the dog to get the full weight of their body behind them in a forward direction. They just do not have the leverage necessary to pull you forward anymore. If your dog will wear this, I believe it to be the most important piece of equipment you can own for a dog that pulls.

Captain in Rock Creek Park using a Halti Head Collar.

Easy Walk

Similar in simple construction to the Gentle Leader, this is meant to be worn around the chest and underbelly and across the back of the dog. It is typically made of nylon with options to attach a lead to the chest or back. I would recommend attaching the bolt snap to the front harness to reduce pulling. These are meant to redirect his attention back to you when he starts to pull. As he pulls away, the tension of the leash will guide him toward the end of the lead you are holding, which will keep him/her from pulling away any farther. Some of these styles of harnesses are made with an additional strap that connects the chest strap to the underbelly strap and sits vertically between the legs to ensure the dog can't slip loose. I've had dogs stop cold mid-run, back up, and pop loose. Given the level of flight risk your dog is, this can shoot terror at a million watts through your body. If they don't have the overwhelming desire to flee, count your blessings and (tighten it) slip it back on! It hasn't happened often, but it is handy to know should you find yourself running with a new dog that isn't familiar with you, or you just haven't built the relationship to the point where he understands you're looking out for his safety.

Penny in Rock Creek Park wearing a front attach Easy Walk Harness.

No-Pull Harness (padded)

This type of harness wraps around the chest and underbelly of the dog and latches on either the side or back where the lead attaches. No-pull harnesses are designed with a front attachment point on the chest or a rear attachment point on the spine in the middle of the back. There are also harnesses with both to give you options depending on your activity. Like any choice, each has its merits and drawbacks. For the front attach, you will have a greater amount of control of your dog when needed, especially in cases of sudden redirection. A drawback would be when they are running out in front of you the leash has a tendency to be pulled back and around the shoulder of the dog and to your hand. This could lead to discomfort if they continue to pull for long periods or go running frequently. A case for the rear attach is that the leash does stay clear and is easy to clip on; additionally, there is a mechanism similar to the martingale collar that clinches the vest around the body of the dog when pulled back. The drawback of this specific setup, in my opinion, is the pulling force causes no discomfort since it's distributed more broadly across the chest and body of the dog, which encourages them to pull more.

Bryan and Jade running with a no-pull harness.

Photo by Nick Wignall

Canicross

This very well-built harness is a deluxe version of the body harness with sturdiness, allowing the weight of an object—sled or, in our case, a runner—to be distributed evenly across the body and allow for maximum comfort when pulling. This is designed to let the dog pull you and is optimal for people who want to run fast with their dogs in competition, whether that be a dog-friendly 5K, Canicross, or dog sledding. Be advised, if the conditions are anything less than dry and perfect, you will fall. Honestly, you are probably going to fall anyway, but the people who use these for competition understand that pushing your limits means potentially exceeding them for glory, and occasionally, for pain.

Dog Pulling When Walking

Sometimes people can be scared of running with dogs who pull when they walk. To them, I say, running is your friend!

Six years into running with packs of dogs and the hardest part is still the pre-run shake-out walk. It is probably equal parts anticipation and restlessness. I've noticed that once you're out the door, it can be challenging to get their attention focused. Just know that it is natural for them to be a bit unfocused. They're experiencing all the smells and sounds, so they need a moment to acclimate to their surroundings. They'll also want to sniff and mark and zigzag across the sidewalk while catching sight of the random rodent who has taken up residence in the tree in front of your home.

Exercise patience because this is necessary, get all this distracted energy out, and let them use the restroom. Work up a slow trot for a quarter of a mile and let them get into their groove. Sometimes they'll want to turn back home and hesitate, but eventually something in their brain switches and the run turns into their work. When they have a job to do, the focus is incredible! It feels as if a switch is flipped and they are very business-like. Like most areas, there are some who are better suited to staying focused. Once on the run, your job is to stay alert to the surroundings and prevent surprises where possible. If you see a blind corner coming up, move the dog to the wide side of the turn. If dogs are coming and they are off-leash while you are leashed, check that ego and pull over to let them pass. Always put you and your dog in a position to continue on enjoying the run.

Night Running

The most important factor is visibility! First, that you are visible to others, and second, that your path is visible to you and your dog. Short of lighting yourself up like a Christmas tree, which I highly recommend you do and share on Instagram, you can use wearable lights that won't disrupt your run but will help others see you. If you are not a big fan of holding things or using lights, many companies now make athletic wear that have reflectors built into them for night-time running. But the absolute most important thing is that you slow down and remain alert of others. Remember that just because you see them does not mean that they see you. When running at night, I strongly discourage running with music or any other sound in your ears. You are already operating with one diminished sense (sight), so making sure the other four are available will keep you safer. Being able to hear can alert you to the footsteps of another runner coming from behind or a distracted driver that hasn't seen you. Helping them see you and your dog is key to remember, too. You might assume that you would have your bases covered by outfitting yourself, but it is equally important to make your dog visible. Eyes will be directed to the items they can see and identify. If they see you, they may only give you enough space for what they think is a runner. If you have a dog who isn't visible on a six-foot leash, they honestly may not see them and not give you AND your dog enough space as they pass. Your goal is to run safely at night, and there are two important measures to maintain: making sure others can see you and making sure you can see where you are going.

Running Vests

If you find yourself by schedule or by desire often logging miles in the dark, I would consider reflective vests a must-have for you and your dog. The goal here is to increase both you and your dog's visibility to others during low-light runs. These vests are brightly colored, usually orange or yellow, and have reflective material sewn in or embedded in the design of the garment. They are typically mesh and lightweight, making storage and transportability easy. Having one for your dog as well as yourself makes certain that any oncoming traffic can see you and your running partner. They light up your body well to give the passerby a good idea of who is running by. They make them for both runners and dogs and are a very helpful tool.

Running Shirts | Jackets

Whatever your most outer layer is for your run, find something with the reflective technology built in. If you don't like the feeling of a vest moving all around as you run, grabbing a shirt or jacket that has the capability to get the attention of others is great. (A nice thing about reflective clothing is that it solves a problem that a lot of people care about, so lots of money has gone into solving it.) You aren't limited to the orange and yellow of the vest, since the reflective material is brought into the design of the garment itself. If looking "cool" while you run is something that is important to you, you'll appreciate the care and time devoted to this solution.

Light-Up Collars | Leashes | Wearables

These are all self-explanatory, but their value in creating visibility is high. They won't necessarily help you with seeing the ground or the stability of your footing, but they do assist in helping others see you. The collars have a solid white or neon color that will have a setting that allows them to stay on constantly or flash, and the same goes for the leashes. Again, it is just as important that drivers, cyclists, and other night runners can see your dog. Wearables is a catch-all term

I mean to substitute for glowing or light-up necklaces, harnesses, or the light-up cords that can be clasped around your dog's torso.

Pepper Spray | Mace

Speaking of safety, to ignore that it is more dangerous running at night would be willfully ignorant and a disservice to you. Maybe that's part of the reason you have a dog, to accompany you on your nighttime runs? In the event that your Fido can't turn into Cujo when you need him to, it is a great idea to carry a handheld deterrent for emergency use. If you don't want to carry it, clip it to your shorts, belt, or shirt. It's a minor tax on the ability to retrieve it quickly to help neutralize a potential threat.

These have all been solutions for night running, but as we mentioned previously, that is only half of the goal. Being able to see where you are going is also helpful in completing night runs safely. In an urban setting you'll be aided in this by lights at intersections, storefronts, or street-lights, but to those of you who like to run the trails, seeing your footing on trails, even if not technical, can be a huge service to you avoiding twisted ankles and tripping over those pesky roots and rocks.

Flashlights for Running

Headlamp

This is my favorite solution for flashlights on the run. I'm a fan of the headlamp because the beam of light is shining from the middle of your forehead, meaning that where your head is pointed your light is shining. With a slight tilt of your head, your path will be well illuminated, and the light source will stay relatively consistent while keeping the ability to look and light things that are not the trail directly in front of you.

Chest Mount

This is also a fantastic solution for helping you see in the dark on trails or roads. If it is a directional light, you can point it at the trail to see obstacles, or you can just light the general area in front of you. It disperses the light a little more widely so others can see you well, too. It may also be the most comfortable of the solutions. Some runners don't like the extra weight of a headlamp, and this option is usually built to wrap around your chest and shoulders, making the weight negligible. There is a little bounce in the light if it is not designed well, so keep that in mind when making a decision.

Handheld

A handheld flashlight is low on the list for functionality. Yes, it does get the job done, but it is much more active in practice because you either have to alter your natural stride to keep the roadway lit properly, or live with the fact that your swinging arm is only going to light the path ahead of you every other stride. Add to that a dog leash in your alternate hand, and you'll find yourself quickly running out of useful hands for anything else that you may need, like a water bottle.

Hydration

Hydration Backpacks

I expand on these further in the Summer section of the book, but I think the solution they offer of being able to deliver water on long runs without being too hand-dependent is a major bonus. Being able to turn your head to the side and quench your thirst is invaluable when you have a leash in one hand and maybe another object—like a light—in your other. More deluxe versions are built with pockets and compartments to store all manner of things for you and your dog—keys, wallet, phone, snacks for you and your dog, and a basic first aid kit.

Water Belt

This is a good solution if you don't want to have to stop on your runs for water. Water belts allow you to carry water bottles without having to hold them in your hands or store them on the route under a bush or behind a tree. You know you've done it. They typically carry two to four bottles distributed around the waist, meaning you can fill one with a replenishing fluid and not be beholden to water only. The drawback is that there can be a bit of bounce, making the run uncomfortable if the belt is not engineered well. Some belts have claimed to solve this, but I've yet to find one that eliminates the problem entirely.

Handheld Water Bottle

There are specialty water bottles made for runners. The runner can slide their hand into the wrap in order to carry the bottle on the run. This is a fantastic hydration solution for a runner, but for running with a dog, it can compromise the one free hand you have if you are holding the leash in the other. This becomes a much more viable solution if you are using a hands-free leash.

Neon is your friend! Say it with me, "Neon is my friend!" Your mission while running at night should be to look like a highlighter.

Always, always, always, leash up at night. This is non-negotiable. Typically, you can get your dog's attention if you see the squirrel first. But in the dark, all bets are off, and his nose is better than your eyes in the dark. The last thing you want is a dog going full ninja assassin on wild rodents when cars can't see him well.

It is also important to think about your lighting, hydration, and leash solutions as one puzzle that you'll need to think about as a whole. What tools are going to work in concert together? If you decide on a hydration backpack, look for one with reflective material built in and understand you'll likely need a headlamp or handheld lighting option. If you prefer water bottles and handheld lamps, you will be required to use a hands-free leash option. All of this is manageable, but finding the best overall solution may mean sacrificing the best option in each particular category. Find the items that help you complete the runs with your dogs safely and with confidence.

Bryan with Lentil and Cleo.

Photo by Chris Roden

CHAPTER FIVE:
Who Shouldn't Run and When Not to Run

As discussed in previous chapters, running with your dog can be a great solution for anxiety, helping the dog become healthier through weight loss, relieving boredom and energy, and as a shared activity that will help build a solid relationship between you and your dog. However, there are a few situations where the benefits of running with your dog are outweighed by the safety concerns.

In "Chapter 2: Assessing Your Dog for the First Time," I mentioned I would strongly discourage any long-distance running with any dog that is younger than twelve months and, in some cases, up to fifteen months of age. Puppy energy can sometimes be overwhelming for a new dog owner to deal with. I haven't done any real analysis of this phenomenon, but I am fairly certain that there is an inverse relationship between the energy and time you have, to the time and energy your puppy requires and, in some instances, needs. We've all seen the constant struggles of balancing training, feeding schedules, and the planning of requisite walks for potty breaks. That's before we factor in the demands of your job and/or family! Now add on to that your puppy has been outfitted with an energy source rivaled only by the sun, and you think you have found the solution in running. I beg of you, proceed with caution!

Equally important is learning when your dog has advanced in age to the point that running is no longer going to be a beneficial habit for them. Being aware of the decline in energy, muscle tone, and stamina as your dog ages can help you begin to scale back the running, both in distance and frequency. Something to pay attention to is the recovery time they need to resume their normal behavior after a run. If your dog is taking longer and longer to bounce back after a run, think about reducing the distance or pace. Pay close attention to the season; the same effort and distance in the spring may decline during the summer months because of the temperatures. If that is the case, you'll see the stamina pick back up in the fall.

Generally speaking, you'll begin to notice the decline as they approach nine years of age. At this point, the warmup before your run is important to remember and observe. Keep an eye out for any limping or hitches in their gait. Also, as they age you will start to notice them fatiguing earlier in the run. I would recommend keeping the same duration but slowing down the pace. Beyond that, think about adding an extra rest day to their routine.

In this chapter, I'll also be discussing the specific instances and breeds where running for extended periods of time can result in undue stress, whether that be caused by their diminished capacity to cool themselves or other internal and even external factors.

Running is a fantastic exercise solution for dogs, but learning the phrase, "All dogs can run, but it is up to you to learn how far and how fast it can be done safely," is just as important to ensuring they can continue to run, which will in turn keep them healthy and happy. We will help you understand the situations where long-distance running is not the solution and suggest a few alternatives that may help until the day they are capable of running, if and when that exists.

Gwynne with Oskar running across the steps of The United States Supreme Court.

Photo by Chris Roden

Who Shouldn't Run

Younger Than Twelve Months (Sometimes Fifteen)

The major concern here is the physical development and maturation of the dog. When dogs are younger, their growth plates are working in overdrive. Look at pictures of puppies at two to three months versus seven to eight months old. In a short period (four to six months) the size and weight of your dog can double. During this aggressive growth phase, a dog's joints can become stressed from the growth alone. It is imperative that you remain vigilant to any additional stress you may be causing during this time. You may have already guessed it, but running is one of the ways you could be adding stress.

I've mostly been talking about structural stressors to the musculoskeletal system, but I should also point out that the cardiovascular system isn't quite primed either. The repetitive striking of the pavement during running is what is going to cause injury. The cardiovascular system is also something that needs to be developed, so it's important that you continue to be your dog's advocate.

All of the communication between you and your dog is non-verbal, aside from the occasional whine, or yelp, to get your attention for some pain point. It's more common that your dog will be ready to charge off during the runs and do their best to remain by your side. When they are young, this can cause an unnatural gate that can lead to the structural problems already discussed. Their bodies aren't efficient in cooling themselves, and they can be at risk for overexertion and heatstroke.

Brachycephalic

These are dogs with a shortened muzzle. These dogs are poor candidates to run longer distances because their ability to cool their internal temperature is less efficient, which can lead to respiratory distress. A natural reaction to increased running is the internal temperature increasing as the run continues, and being able to continually cool the air becomes more important. The most efficient mechanism for regulating body temperature is cooling the air at intake through the nose.

Generally speaking, the longer the snout, the more efficiently the air that enters the body can be cooled. With brachycephalic dogs, their nose is very short and almost smushed; the nostrils can be narrow, and just taking in enough air can be problematic. You may have noticed that they snort, have noisy breath, and get tired much quicker during walks and exercise; these are all common experiences with brachycephalic dogs. Some of the more popular breeds include Boxers, Bulldogs, Boston Terriers, Pugs, Shih Tzus, and King Cavalier Spaniels.

Running with Boxers

Honestly, most of the time when people contact us about running with their dogs they've done some research and usually self-select. Families aren't too concerned about getting their Pug out on a run. They've seen how these brachycephalic dogs respond to the slightest exertion of energy and how long it can sometimes take them to stop the panting afterward. These types of dogs are best suited with a short jog no longer than a block at a time and mixed into their morning, mid-day, or evening walks. The most common brachycephalic dog breed that we are contacted about is the Boxer. These fantastic dogs are incredibly athletic, with great build and muscle tone and more than enough energy. The only thing holding them back is the shortened muzzle. If I could put an asterisk on the brachycephalic breeds, it would be the Boxer. Due to the shortened muzzle, they do lack stamina and are prone to overheat. I would say running with Boxers would be a soft yes. But only if you have the capacity to run with them solo in order to give them your full attention. Even then, I would strongly discourage running in the summer months if you live in the southern half of the country where mornings can climb into the 80s just after the sun rises.

As a rule, our company does not take on Boxers as runners because our small pack group runs do not allow for the necessary supervision a Boxer requires. Being hyper-vigilant about the weather and conditions are other concerns with these dogs. Since they have trouble regulating internal temperatures, they are much more sensitive to the runs during warmer months. Contrast that with their short hair, and they aren't well suited to frolic in the subfreezing temperatures of the winter months of northern states. The conditions need to be between the high 40s and mid-70s for the best results. Of course there are exceptions to the rule, but I think keeping in mind these standards will make for the best and safest experiences.

Canine Hip Dysplasia

This is a hereditary condition more commonly found in larger dogs but can occur in smaller dogs, as well. It is an issue originating in the hip sockets of the rear legs. A properly functioning hip comprises a ball and socket joint that glides smoothly with a natural range of motion. In cases where hip dysplasia is present, there is an issue caused by the ball and socket not fitting properly. The components can grind or rub, causing deterioration over time. This condition can be diagnosed as early as four months old. It can also be exacerbated with too much exercise. In short, the impact of running habitually will cause the hip to be overused and either not develop properly or wear out sooner because of the stress. This is a primary factor of why veterinarians and other dog professionals, including myself, are adamant about not running puppies. The indicators that your puppy may have hip dysplasia are decreased activity and range of motion; difficulty jumping, running, or climbing stairs; pain and stiffness; an unnatural gait when running; and they usually have a looping hop or hitch in their movement while running rather than the smooth glide.

Older Dogs

Any dogs older than nine years that have not already been running long distances through their maturing years should not start running, at least not to the level we've been primarily discussing. The physiology of elder dogs is different and on the decline, so a short trot may be what is best. Their muscles and bone density and structure have changed, and their bounce-back may not be what it once was. I would recommend at least a day of rest, or more, as the standard for elder dogs who are already accustomed to running. I think at best, late age dogs who begin running need to run no more than twice a week, and it should not be with any major goal in mind, but just to have some fun. At this age, maintenance is the most important function running can serve. Going for a couple runs a week can still be helpful in decreasing health risks such as arthritis, heart conditions, and obesity. Keeping the exercise light will also help with reducing inflammation, helping blood flow, and keeping muscles, joints, and ligaments strong.

When Not to Run

Extreme Heat

Modifications are required when the temperatures start reaching the mid-80s. Depending on the climate, whether it's dry in the Southwest or humid in the Mid-Atlantic, not all heat is the same. We'll get more into the specific solutions of regions later in the book, but knowing when to call off a run can be life-saving. Dogs, like humans, can train to be more resilient in hot conditions and some specific breeds are better disposed to running in the heat.

But for those not on the extremes, heat can be a serious threat to safety. A short dog physiology lesson: Dogs do not sweat; they pant to cool the air that they take in. If the air is too hot or they are needing to pant too much, the system can become overstressed and not function properly.

Dulce showing the aftereffects of a moderate run on a warm day.

Signs of Heatstroke

Most of the signs will come from the snout and mouth. Heavy panting will increase as heatstroke progresses. They begin to drool or salivate more than usual. The tongue will turn bright red and their gums can do the same or go pale. The heart rate will increase, and breathing can become distressed. They may become irritable, agitated, or restless.

Here's what to do if you think your dog is having a heatstroke:

- Do your best to get them to a cooler, climate-controlled setting. Your car with the AC on, or if you are not near your car, knock on a door if you are in a neighborhood. Get bold, there is no time for shyness in moments like these.
- Water is your friend. If you are near a fresh body of water, let your dog take a dip. If not, find water and get it on their body. If you can't do that, use cool, wet cloths or towels to wipe the neck, armpits, and between the hind legs.
- If he is able to drink, give him cool water. DO NOT add ice or feed him ice directly. This can cause shock by lowering the body temperature too rapidly.
- Call your vet, or the nearest one to you, and begin driving there. Let them know the situation so they can be prepared to take action as you arrive.

Apart from the air temperature, the heat of the surface you are running on is equally important. The most dangerous time of day to run with your dog from a heat standpoint is between 5 p.m. and sundown during warm sunny days. The sun has had the chance to beat down on the pavement and sidewalks, heating them up all day. Even if the temperatures don't seem too humid or hot for a run, it is always vital that you check the ground temperature. Using the back side of your hand, press it to the ground and hold it. If after five to ten seconds it becomes too uncomfortable to keep it down, do your best to find another place to run. Find a shaded trail that has had the luxury of a shaded canopy covering it.

Bryan running with Fayde and Jade in
Highland Park, Texas.

Photo by Nick Wignall

If you don't heed the warning, be aware of a condition known as
tenderfoot. This happens when the pads of a dog's feet are burned or
injured because of ground temperature. It could also be a blister or
cut, but avoiding hot pavement during the hottest months is the best
way to protect their pads.

Something to think about, especially for urban dwellers, are dog
boots. It can be tough to avoid pavement for you, and driving out
to a trail may be a great solution for a weekend run, but going out
during the week is still an issue. They definitely take a little getting
used to for your dog, but prioritizing function over aesthetics will
keep you on the roads running! You'll recognize it when the dog is
hobbling or walking very gingerly on the affected foot. They'll have
a hard time bearing any weight and will hop around. If you check

the rest of the leg and nothing bothers them, it is likely tenderfoot. (Additional remedies discussed in "Chapter 6: Seasonal Running Solutions.")

Extreme Cold

Weather conditions are a constant variable for running with your dog. The temperatures alone don't always dictate a good day for running. It is imperative that you factor in the wind. January 21, 2019, will live in infamy around these parts! It broke our streak of 1,774 days of not being canceled by the weather. We do our best to live up to the moniker of being all-weather runners, but even that day was just a bit too much in the Washington, DC, area. The temperature was in the low teens, which honestly wouldn't have been enough to shut down our long-haired dogs. Our short-haired dogs typically bottom out around the 20-degree mark. If the family hasn't already canceled, I'll give my best evaluation of safety and convince them that maybe a bathroom break at most is enough and do my best to get the dogs out for a run as soon as possible, even if that means adding runs. What made this particular day with low teen temperatures unbearable was the combination of frigid temperatures and twenty-mile-per-hour winds. Short of professionally trained Huskies who live in that weather for most of the year and have acclimated to it, I would strongly discourage trying to go for a run. Yes, there are great solutions and smart technology for runners to help regulate and offset the temperatures by layering up and adding gloves and specialized socks and winter hats. But at best, we can offer our dogs a windbreaker that is more for rain and does very little to help them on runs.

If being miserable isn't enough to dissuade you, again, be aware of the dangers of tenderfoot. This can be caused by getting the pads wet and running on the cold surfaces. The pads are sensitive, and you'll see the dog begin to hobble and limp during or after exercises. The grass and other surfaces have less give during colder weather as it hardens, and that, too, can irritate the paws and cause damage or injury.

Lentil, Scout, Louie, Nova, and Cleo posing on The National Mall.

Tennis Courts

Avoid tennis courts at all costs. Although they really do seem like a great spot for dogs—high fences and enclosed areas that get very little use in off-season or bad weather make it seem like a fantastic place to get the dog off-leash and do a little fetch or running around—the surfaces on a tennis court are made specifically to create friction and allow tennis shoes to stick; this does the same to the pads of your dog's feet. What ends up happening is the dog takes a turn too sharp or an aggressive launch from standing, and the pads grip the court and can rip or tear off completely. This can leave a bloody mess on you, the court, and them. It is painful, and they may have a limp. I strongly discourage tennis courts as a place for them to go for exercise.

This chapter is great for examining the realities of running with your dog and when it may not be the right solution. I fully believe that running is, and can be, a fantastic activity for all dogs, but take into consideration that finding the right time and fit are equally important. Safety is always our primary concern when going for a run, and ensuring that we take the preventative steps necessary is a great way to avoid injury. As always, use your best judgment when taking on the activity, consult your veterinarian, and re-read the parts of this chapter that touch on your concerns. Check your ego and realize that modifying a run is going to be better than exposing your dog to a dangerous situation.

Rather than being discouraged about the fact that you can't run with your dog for one of the reasons described here, think about ways you can get your dog tired that are temporary solutions until they can participate in running safely.

Consider swimming if the season and climate are right for you. Some dogs absolutely love and thrive in the water. Invest in a ball launcher if you don't have a professional-caliber baseball arm. Don't get discouraged, because if you search hard enough, you'll find a solution that will work either temporarily or long-term. Being mindful of your dog's physical and mental health should always be prioritized.

David and Bear on a morning run through Rock Creek Park in Washington, DC.

Photo by Chris Roden

CHAPTER SIX:
Seasonal Running Solutions

I've spent a fair amount of time in Texas, where summers last from April to October (not to mention, the peak months of July to September are basically as hot as the surface of the sun). You get to know that running in the early morning is the only running worth doing. Anything after that should be canceled or left for the next day. If you want to be a hero and pound the pavement in the scorching temperatures, be my guest, but please leave your dog behind. They'll be overworked and miserable if you try to take them for a run when you get home from work. Knowing when to call off a run is the hallmark of a great owner who cares about the long-term health and wellness of their pet.

I've also spent a considerable amount of time running through the four seasons of the Mid-Atlantic. The seasons here on the East Coast are true and blend pretty well. Whether you're a minimalist or a gear lover, running through different weather and conditions will be aided greatly with a little preparation and knowledge. I'll offer recommendations and solutions on what has helped me negotiate the changes in season.

The heat, rain, snow, and sleet can all be conquered with the right plan and execution. Leave the hail and thunderstorm to the weather channel! We're pretty proud runners at DC Dog Runner, and usually, the only thing slowing us down is making sure there is parking near enough for us to grab your dog; we've been known to run appointments when the city is shut down or the streets haven't been plowed!

The saying around here and other more southern climates is true, "It isn't the heat but the humidity that gets you." Although the temperatures don't get too out of control here in DC, topping out around the high 80s most summer days, it will sneak up into the mid-90s on the warmest days. But what is constant is how heavy the air feels because we push up against the Potomac River and the fact that the city was built on a swamp. If I'm being honest, I don't mind a nice summer!

Unless you live in San Diego (shout out to Doggie Joggie) where they have perma-spring, it'll be helpful to know the variables due to weather and how to solve them.

Nicole running with Wookie, Rocco, and Scout through Rock Creek Park in Washington, DC.

Photo by Chris Roden

Spring | Fall

In my opinion, spring and fall are the easier seasons to prepare for.

Spring

The temperatures are mild and the warmth comes on slowly to give you a chance to acclimate. The spring brings a pleasant respite from the harshness of winter, and the only real issue is the once wide-open trails are packed with runners, bikers, walkers, and other dogs. It seems that everyone simultaneously awakes from their winter slumber and the first hint of warm, dry weather brings everyone (and their dog) outside. In a city like DC that is already very active, it means that anywhere you have had the luxury of running freely will now be congested. The city sidewalks have people, who would have normally driven, walking and riding bikes. The monuments are flooded with tourists and families with small children. The trails are no longer dotted with other winter warriors but are now crawling with nature walks, dogs, hikers, and all the good-weather runners.

So, what are you supposed to do? Enjoy it!

Bear, Heidi, and Sam pose near the Basilica of the National Shrine of the Immaculate Conception.

Soak it in. Understand that your pace may suffer a bit, but let the sun shine on your face and use a slightly shorter leash to keep them closer and better navigate the traffic. Bask in the glory that is the second best season, in my humble opinion, to run.

If you still insist on being annoyed, get up earlier; the trails will still be open in the early hours and the busy daytime traffic will not be around, meaning quieter streets; the shops and brunch spots don't open until later in the morning, so the sidewalks will be clear. Do your best to solve your own dissatisfaction by changing your routine.

Fall

For similar reasons to spring, fall is a wonderful season and my personal favorite. The temperatures fade from warm in the early part of the season and begin a slow methodical march through cooler weather with a crispness that eventually blends to the frigid temperatures of the winter. It is the slow, gradual drop of the air that gives you time to enjoy and embrace the chilly months approaching. You find that one day you wake up and you grab the long-sleeved shirt instead of just the T-shirt, or you grab a hoodie to add a layer. You'll notice that by the end of the season, the trails begin to decongest and the sidewalks are a little more clear each weekend. There are really no barriers to running with your dog in the fall once the calendar turns to November. Even the sight lines during your runs begin to open up. The opacity of the trees with their leaves give way to the bare, stripped branches, giving you a glimpse into the depths of the woods you are running through. The sky may be overcast more often than not with the threat of showers constantly looming. It is a nice buffer to have between the scorching sun of summer and the harsh frozen ground of winter.

Trails tend to be a little more uniform in the fall due to the yellow, red, brown, and orange leaves carpeting the forest ground. It can hide roots and rocks that were uncovered during the spring and summer. The worry is sprained ankles and other potential injuries from falling due to unstable footing. You'll want to focus much more on the five to seven feet in front of you.

Because they are so similar, a lot of the solutions are the same, so I've decided to combine information where I can and make notes for changes where necessary.

Rain

I've always thought it fun to run in the rain. I stand by that statement, but I've sort of amended it to, "Getting wet sucks, but once you are wet, running can be really fun." Especially with the proper gear, running in the rain can be very engaging and mentally stimulating. You will need to listen to your dog and gauge how they feel about the run and carry an extra towel or two in your car. A good investment would be a backseat cover; they are made for cars and SUVs and can be a lifesaver when it comes to combatting the smell of wet dog dominating your car for the next week and beyond.

Lentil, Scout, Bear, and Captain in the rain.

If you do plan on trail running, grabbing your dog a raincoat can help, too. I tend to go without them, but some dogs like it. Grab them something that is form-fitting with high-quality fastening. It should not restrict movement but it also should not be so loose that you spend half of your time adjusting and re-adjusting until it's just better to run without. As with all dog gear, if it gives you a headache, it is not the solution.

As for yourself, there are fantastic options for raincoats, but my favorite has to be the **Patagonia Houdini**. Its best quality is that it bunches up and folds into its own chest pocket. It is lightweight and will keep you dry on a thirty-minute-or-less run. This is a fantastic option on confusing days that rain may or may not be predicted, because you can keep it on you without it taking up too much space or adding too much weight. If rain is in the forecast, then bringing along something with **Gore-Tex** will be your best friend. It keeps me dry on runs longer than thirty minutes. You will sweat, so take advantage of the venting options provided. I like these two because they are high-quality, high-value, durable jackets that have lasted many seasons. You can go higher-end like **Arc'teryx** or get lucky with a cheaper option, as well. As always, no one jacket serves everyone, so find what makes you feel good while running, and be confident about it!

Shoes

There is of course a case to be made for enjoying the rain and just allowing yourself to get soaked. Adopt the mentality of running in the rain as a challenge. When you approach it that way, the squelching of waterlogged socks and shoes won't bother you as much. The clothes clinging to your body as you soak up mile after mile become a natural coolant to the overheating body. Be ready to slow down with your dog, at least in the beginning of your run, to get used to your footing.

If you are a puddle jumper or run through standing water, having shoes that fit and that will not give you blisters is a must. Additionally, if you decide to go with your dog to the trails, consider investing in some trail-specific running shoes. These shoes are specially designed and have a harder kickplate, making it a bit more rigid but saving your foot from sharp roots potentially piercing through your shoe. They also have deeper grooves in the tread to give you better traction and feel.

On the other hand, your dog was built for running like this. You'll likely see more playfulness and exuberance from them. They have the advantage of two extra legs for stabilizing and running quickly and on balance. There are some dogs who just hate any weather and won't run or even want to go outside. If this is the case for you and your dog, give them a rest and head out on your own.

Bryan with Lentil and Huxley.

Hats

- **Beanies:** Finding a lightweight beanie made of polyester with some elasticity will be comfortable and not make you sweat on longer runs. Most days during spring/fall you won't need it, but it's nice to have the option if you end up wanting to run before the sun rises or after nightfall.

- **Running hats:** A nice running hat is made of similar material, polyester and spandex, for a nice fit that will not irritate. It should have wicking technology and have a breathable crown so as not to take on weight or create excess sweat on your head. The running hat is a fantastic solution if you don't care for sunglasses but want to block the sun from your eyes on a run. Finding a hat can be a difficult process because heads come in all shapes and sizes, so try them on and find a fit and style you like.
- **Visor:** A variation of the running hat—it's basically a convertible. This allows the maximum breathability because of the open crown, while keeping the sun off of your face and eyes. Visors are also helpful in keeping the sweat from dripping down into your eyes.

Winter

Colder temperatures and inclement weather are a fact of life in this season. I've always thought that the worst running weather is temperatures in the high thirties and raining. Running in the cold can be mitigated with proper layering. Running in the rain can be offset with the proper gear and attitude. Mixing them together and having cold, wet clothes and shoes are about as bad as it can get. At least when it snows, the scenery gets a bit of a facelift. The brown turns to a winter wonderland. In the (almost) freezing rain, brown turns to muddy brown, and you just get cold, then wet, then dirty. The End.

Accessories

- **Beach towel:** A what? Do you have your seasons confused? No, but a beach towel is a necessary accessory for winter runs. During the winter your dog will track in everything from the outside. Purchasing a large beach towel in addition to your blanket or back seat cover will save you headache and heartache, not to mention your olfactory senses.

- **Baby wipes:** They'll help with cleaning your dog's feet before tracking snow and dirt and grime through your car or home. It's a nice way to also clean any toxic chemicals used to keep roadways clear of snow (more on that in the next section). They are super versatile to have in general if you have a dog, and getting in the habit of cleaning and checking their pads will keep them on the roads and trails.

Snow

Running in the snow is similar in ways to running in the rain, with the caveat that you may not see roots and rocks that have iced over.

Lentil, Tahoe, Gracie, Nova, Bear, Scout, and Heidi trail running Sugar Loaf Mountain in Maryland.

Core, leg, and arm strength working in concert will keep you from falling over. The major concern is reducing injury caused by slipping and falling during snow and icy conditions. The snow actually provides a nice crunch under your shoes that can be negotiated comfortably if the surface is flat.

If you plan on running with elevation changes, how you ascend and descend with a dog is important. Stay alert and take steps carefully until you get your footing. This goes for your dog, as well. Your dog will adapt to the conditions more quickly, but keep him close to you and try not to run out of control. I recommend short, choppy steps ascending and it may be worth considering walking the descents. Twisted ankles, stretched groins, and sprained wrists are all at risk because of the slippery conditions.

Some major concerns for urban runners are the preparations cities make in salting and working to de-ice roadways and sidewalks. In some cases, these can be toxic and stick to the pads and webbing between your dog's toes. If your dog is a true dog, he'll want to lick them clean. Ingesting these chemicals can be harmful and poisonous, which can lead to sickness and a trip to the emergency room.

Tips

- **Musher's Secret®:** You can apply this wax as a preventative barrier before going out on the run to protect your dog's pads from salt residue, ice buildup, and tenderfoot. Get in the habit of applying it two to three times per week so the pads are always protected in the event you forget before going out the door! Rubbing it in will create and maintain a protective barrier on the foot. It is made from 100 percent food grade natural wax. Whether you prefer the trail paths or the harsher city sidewalks and roads, this is a must-have item to keep you running together and without injury.
- **Runner rules:** Grab a high-quality pair of running shoes with deep tread, and if possible, a guard to keep snow out of the

Nova at The Wharf in SW Washington, DC, after a good snow.

inside. Doing your best to keep socks dry or even bringing an extra pair will keep you going stronger and longer. If you are hesitant to buy specialty trail-running shoes because of the cost, I would recommend researching Yaktrax. This is a traction device you attach externally to the bottom of your standard running shoe; it is made of high-quality rubber, steel spikes, and steel coils. These are a fantastic option if you switch shoes often or would like the option, too. They have a large selection, but the best options for running are the "Run" and "Pro" models.

Sleet

You don't know sleet is a problem until you are caught in it. Rain turns to sleet in the blink of an eye at the right temperatures, and you can feel it. Everything gets slick. This is another great spot to slip on your Yaktrax, but slowing down especially on pavement will be your best course of action. It can be hard to tell when a slick spot develops. I find it best to run on the grass as much as possible when it is sleeting—there tends to be a bit more traction to keep you upright and moving forward. Check your ego and take short, choppy steps, and do your best not to lean.

Sleet can hurt when coming down, so consider wearing gloves, tights, or pants, and even a face mask or guard. The idea is to protect any exposed skin because frozen hands will ultimately mean a diminished grip on the leash, and if you are too focused on the pain of running in the sleet, you won't be paying attention to your dog.

I also recommend taking breaks. Stop every mile or so and brush your dog off so the icicles don't accumulate in the webbing between their toes or on their fur. It may not bother them, but it can be painful for them if it builds up and rests between their toes. The same goes for around their eyes and ears. Dogs aren't nearly as bothered by inclement weather as we are, but we always need to keep their health and safety at the top of our mind when taking them out.

Gear for Dogs

- **Jacket:** If you have a long-haired dog, honestly, they are well-suited to the cold, and I wouldn't bother with a vest, sweater, or jacket, because the return on investment is minimal. They were built to run in colder temperatures, so save yourself the hassle. If you run with a short-haired dog, there are great options for them, and they are numerous. Depending on if you primarily appreciate the form or functionality will lead you down separate roads. I'm more concerned with the fit than the style or materials. It is not a useful or helpful tool if you spend more time adjusting it.

- **Dog boots, dog socks, or dog shoes:** a rose by any other name—whatever you call them, these are useful accessories for your dog. Half the battle is getting them on without your dog shaking them free. Next is watching them walk around like a newborn fawn as they try to understand what is on their feet.

But then they become comfortable in them and are off to the races. Like shoes for you, they come with multiple fits and tread patterns. Some of the creative small distributors have even made mock UGGS® and Chuck Taylor's®, but for running, the straight-forward, runner-soled, nylon upper with Velcro® straps will be your best bet. These can look a little funny, but they are a nice tool and less maintenance than the continual application and clean-up of "Musher's Secret."

Lentil, Bella, Scout, Captain, and Diesel pose in front of Duke Ellington School of the Arts.

Gear for Runners

- **Gloves:** You should use gloves that keep your hands warm during the run without causing you to sweat. Most brands make a touchscreen-compatible fingertip that allows you to control your phone without taking off the glove. I have two styles; one pair is thinner with a retractable water- and wind-proof mitt that tucks into a fold in the glove. I like this for rainy days, when temperatures are cold but not below freezing, or when it is windy. They are semi-fitted, meaning your fingers can continue to move freely. This is a great option when you need to pick up after your dog but don't want to take your glove off to do so. The second pair is thicker but with individual fingers to maintain dexterity. They are best for temperatures below freezing and allowing you to keep a strong grip on leashes. The only issue is having to pull them off when scooping the poop!

- **Pants:** Depending on your style and desire, there are three options for runners:

  1. The pants that fit more loosely to be slipped on over running shorts.
  2. Tighter form-fitting pants that are a substitute for running shorts.
  3. Compression-fit tights to be worn under your shorts to give you an extra layer.

Whatever your taste, they all perform similar functions in giving you an added layer of protection from the elements. Rather than soaking through your shorts immediately, they can give you a little buffer of time, and if made from tightly woven polyester, they will keep you dry and running.

- **Hats:** I have two different weight performance beanies. The lighter weight one works great for temperatures above freezing. It breathes well and doesn't cause you to sweat as much. The

Bryan with Cleo on a muddy, rainy day in Battery Kemble Park.

heavier weight one is lined and works best to block the wind for temperatures below freezing. Keeping the head and ears warm on longer runs is essential, and a nice hat that doesn't irritate will make the experience so much better.

- **Mask:** For the extremely cold and windy days, I use a ¾ mask that I can zip-tighten around the back. It has a breathable mesh portion for the mouth and nose and works well as a neck warmer when you don't want it around your face. There are also full over-the-head options that protect the neck, and for the hardest of hardcore runners, the mask with only eye holes may be your jam!

Summer

In the summer, it is important to pay attention to your dog's tongue, panting, and pacing. Watching the tongue is the first step in assessing your dog's condition on the move. They are likely running with their mouth open. If they are in fantastic condition or are naturally fit for running, you may not be able to see the tongue because they are efficient at cooling the air.

When the tongue is outside their mouth but it's darting in and out rhythmically with their panting, there is no need to panic or take action. Your dog has it under control and is not distressed in any measurable way. This is the default setting for typical dogs on the run. Even if their breaths are short, focus on the tongue and their control of it. If it looks good, continue with the run as normal.

However, if their tongue is extended outside their mouth and is not going back inside, they are showing the first signs of duress— the tongue is hanging more loosely to one side of the mouth and is flopping around. If they do not seem to have control of it, this is your sign to back off of the run and take a walk break. Find shade if possible and give them a chance to take water and regroup. If you push through this, you run the risk of heatstroke. Your dog's body is giving you a clear indication that it is overworking, and you could be risking serious injury. STOP! I can't stress this enough. Be your pet's safety advocate, and check your ego.

Interval Training

Summer is the perfect time to start mixing in interval training. This is useful because it gives your dog an opportunity to build cardio-vascular fitness and muscle, and it gives you more frequent opportunities to assess your dog because you do not zone out as you can on longer runs. You'll likely be more engaged and in tune with the needs of your dog, and they are less likely to overheat, while still getting a good workout.

Giving up control of the run can be difficult. You'll need to pay closer attention to the non-verbal communication your dog is giving. Ignoring this could land you in the emergency room with an overworked and overheated dog. Knowing when to call off the dogs, pun absolutely intended, is a hallmark of a fantastic owner. Yes, it may mean not getting the mileage in for your prescribed training plan, but miles can be made up. Remember, the goal is to have a long-term running buddy that will age gracefully with health and strength.

Lisa running through Alexandria cobblestones.

Photo by Chris Roden

Handling Ground Temperature

- **Heat hand check:** How hot is too hot? The best low-tech way to gauge the surface temperature is to kneel down and press the back of your hand to the ground. If you can comfortably leave it there for twenty to thirty seconds, it will be OK for the pads of your dog's feet. Asphalt, concrete, and sand all hold heat well and get ample time to warm in the direct sun. Even though the air temperature may be comfortable for a run, it is imperative that you learn the habit of the "heat hand check." As the air temperature decreases later in the day, the ground has been absorbing the rays of the sun for hours and will be its hottest when you are typically returning from work. You risk major injury to your dog's pads, including burning and blistering. You'll see them begin to hobble and limp, unable to bear weight on the extremity.

- **Musher's Secret:** Again, like in the winter section, Musher's can help protect your dog's feet by continuing the same routine of applying two to three times per week. You are trying to protect against hot roads and sidewalks, rough gravel trails, and other potentially unpredictable terrain. Their pads are their first line of defense against injury and will keep them on the road, so it is in our interest to care for them to ensure they are able to get out there with us.

- **Boots, shoes, and socks:** These solutions are helpful in the summertime because they are an extra barrier between your dog's feet and the hot ground. These can be useful in the summers where evenings are long and the sun bakes the pavement even longer. The trails are usually softer, and you can see potential roots, sticks, and rocks, so the boots are primarily for protection against burning. Mind you, if you do have the luxury of having an off-leash runner that leaves the trails, these are great to use to avoid infection from cuts and nicks in the wrong water source.

- **Shade:** Your best friend in the summer is the shade. The longer you can stay under a canopy of trees or behind the shade of buildings, the longer you can stay on the run. The shade has the dual effect of keeping the ground temperature in a safe zone for your dog's feet, and it helps keep the air temperature cooler, which helps everyone on long runs. A shaded trail is the best spot to run during the long summer days.

Cooling

- **Ice vests:** A fantastic tool for dog owners who run. This can extend runs far beyond regular summer distances because it helps keep your dog's core temperature down. There are many kinds that use frozen packs or ice, but my favorite, because of design, function, and size, is the Canine Ice Vest. It has three ways of keeping your dog cool:

  1. Putting ice in the main pockets of the hex mesh pouch so the ice sits against your dog's coat, resulting in an immediate core temperature reduction.
  2. As the ice melts, the water drips down the side of your dog's body, cooling the torso.
  3. The open-air hex mesh design allows for air to circulate under the vest, which allows the temperature to lower through evaporative cooling.

- **CamelBak®:** For the runner, the backpack allows you to fill it with cold ice water and wear with you on your run. It is nice to have access to a water source any time you want instead of having to plan stops around convenience stores or be at the mercy of the urban trail designer's water fountains. A benefit to running with a CamelBak is that you can explore farther away from roads, on longer loops in the woods, and on off-road trails with confidence. If you aren't a fan of holding things in your hands while running, and as a substitute for a dog water bottle, you can use the valve to distribute water into your hands for a DIY bowl that your dog can lap water from.

Investing in a CamelBak is probably the last gear item I adopted that I thought, *You should have bought this way sooner.* I held off because I thought carrying something would weigh and slow me down. There was a short period, about two weeks, of adjustment that took a little getting used to, but after that I was grateful. It was able to hold a cool water source—1.5 liters—but add to that, I was able to take my GU® out of my pockets, my keys from hiding places, my wallet out of my car, my phone off my arm, and it could hold my sunglasses. The extra weight was negligible and absolutely worth it because I was able to keep all my valuables on me during the run, clearing my mind, at least a bit.

An unintended benefit was it allowed me more freedom on longer, ten-plus-mile training runs. I always kept close to major roads in the city because I wanted to be near a water source, and I found myself skipping out on longer trail runs for the same reason. Count me as the converted! I do not like carrying things in my hand, e.g., water bottles, so the camel pack is a great solution. And, it can be an easy way to share water with your dog to drink or pour on them in an emergency situation.

For your dog, there are plenty of water bottle designs that are inexpensive, and it is probably worth finding one that fits your hand so well that you don't notice it at all. I prefer the plastic bottles that have a silicone portion that can wrap around the bottle but be unrolled to create a bowl to squeeze the water into. Keeping one in your hand or on your running belt is a great idea, especially if you are exploring new areas or trails and aren't sure of the availability of water on the run.

Pacing

When first starting with your dog, take it slow. They're just happy to be spending time with you! It is an added bonus that they are running. You're already winning the race, so there is no need to push the pace. That sounded cornier than intended, but hey, it'll be memorable. Use non-verbal cues to let them dictate the pace. Always make sure there is slack in the leash. If they are behind with a taut leash, walk for a bit. Maybe they are just telling you they need to potty, but maybe it is a cue that the pace is a little quick. It is always better to be conservative when beginning. Similarly, if the leash is taut and your dog is out front, it is best to hold them back. The best-case scenario is they run themselves ragged, and you have to carry your dog all the way back to the car/house. You read that right, the BEST scenario! Worst-case scenario your dog ends up with heatstroke.

Heatstroke

Most of the signs will come from the snout and mouth and can include drooling, salivating, a bright red tongue, pale or bright red, and distressed breathing. Heavy panting is common, especially as heatstroke progresses, which can cause them to become disoriented. The heart rate will increase, and the breathing can become further distressed. And finally, they may become irritable, agitated, or restless and may evacuate by vomit or diarrhea. In short, the dog has lost control of his faculties, and the body is doing everything it can to remove heat from the body.

What to Do If You Think Your Dog Is Having a Heatstroke

- Do your best to get them to a cooler setting. Your car, with the air conditioning on. If you are not near your car but are in a neighborhood, knock on a door. Now is the time to put all of your social anxieties aside. People may be taken aback by your request and the urgency of the situation. Time is important, and bargaining with someone who is hesitant to help will only waste it. Have a clear directive for them to understand. Let them know you need a cool home and a tub of cool water to submerge your dog. Move on to the next home if necessary.

- As previously stated, water is your friend. If you are near a fresh body of water, let your dog take a dip, and if you aren't, run water and get it on their body. If you can't do that, use cool wet cloths or towels to wipe the neck, armpits, and between the hind legs.
- If he is able to drink, give him cool water, but DO NOT add ice or feed him ice directly. This can cause shock by lowering the body temperature too rapidly.
- Call your veterinarian, or the nearest one to you, and begin driving there. Let them know the situation so they can be prepared to receive you and take action as soon as you arrive.

Cleo, Lentil, and Mala taking a breather on a steamy day in Rock Creek Park.

Each season brings its own distinct challenges to running, and you probably already have a good idea of which of these extremes you will be subjected to on your runs. Taking the time on the front end to learn the potential dangers and common mistakes will only help you in deciding which tools will be best to help you on your runs. Take your time making a decision and get comfortable with the capabilities, and when in doubt, slow it down a little bit. Do your best to get your bearings in a new situation and get better prepared for the next year. I'm still learning and acquiring more knowledge and gear to help me conquer each season successfully and safely. Enjoy the environment you and your dog get to share as you run through cities or trails in whichever season is upon you.

Megan running with Maximus in Washington, DC.

Photo by Chris Roden

CHAPTER SEVEN:
Urban vs. Trail Running & Single vs. Pack Running

Are you a city slicker or a mountain climber? This is an important distinction in a dog's world. It may mean running in densely populated areas with sights and sounds and smells that can be quite unnerving and require a good bit of discipline and focus. Contrast that with a dog who is paired with an outdoorsman; they'll need to be focused, as well, due to the infinite number of squirrels, rabbits, and ever-elusive white-tail deer! And while the smells and sounds can be less offensive in nature than in the city (street pizza notwithstanding), they are still interesting to a dog and can be distracting when the aim is to hammer out some miles on the softer trails. Clearly, dogs are capable of thriving in most conditions, but setting them and yourself up for success is a nice goal to have.

City dogs will typically need a shorter leash and be comfortable running near their owner to navigate the crowded city streets. Add to that the blind corners, street, sidewalk traffic, and other packs of dogs, and you've got a minefield to negotiate just to get those miles in. It will also be an exercise in patience for you because you will have to do a lot of starting and stopping at stop signs and streetlights, not to mention avoiding any food that may have fallen to the ground that your dog can pick up. Trail dogs usually have the benefit of a little more freedom, and depending on the laws and trust between them and their owner, the ultimate prize: leash-free! Running on trails definitely presents its own challenges and can necessitate running with a little extra gear because of the remoteness of the destinations and distance from immediate medical attention if needed. And still, there are a fair number of dogs who get to spend weekdays in the city and weekends on the trails. Work hard, woof hard, right?

We'll talk about the different conditions and problems different environments present, and our recommendations and solutions on how to run successfully. As usual, it is always about safety first and being able to get out there for more runs!

In addition to this, we'll contrast the solutions for running with a single dog or a pack. The answers in a lot of cases are the same, but there are some nuanced situations that require a different tact, or would be enhanced by a different approach. And last, we'll highlight the specific solutions for running in the dark and how to make yourself more visible to others, as well as tips and tools to keep you safe.

Urban vs. Trail

Sights

- **Urban:** In the city, there is a lot of visual stimulation. Dogs have to contend with commuter traffic, congested sidewalks, signs and signals, storefronts, intersections, buildings, and so much more. It can be a little overwhelming and difficult to concentrate on the task at hand. It is nearly impossible to safely run in an urban setting without a leash. I've seen it attempted, but I would strongly discourage it. Being a good dog owner, you should know that not everyone shares your love and affinity for dogs. Yes, you know your dog is a saint, but there can be something quite unnerving about a seventy-five-pound dog running in your general direction. Keeping your dog focused can be a challenge in this situation, and constant communication and commands will only help with their being able to respond. Of course there is an acclimation period, but dogs are smart animals and adapt to their surroundings. They'll soon be able to block out the distractions and give you their attention. They'll start to learn who along the route leaves treats and water bowls out for them and make a habit of running to them for breaks.

Lisa with Henry navigating a busy sidewalk in Alexandria, Virginia.

Photo by Chris Roden

- **Trail:** While on the surface a little less chaotic for us, nature is filled with sights that can cause a good dog to become a little too curious. With all likelihood, even if you spend a lot of time on trails, you live somewhere more closely resembling the urban city center than the untouched greenery of the forested trails you frequent. Acclimating can take a little time unless there is an off-road trail near you that you become familiar with. In the woods, your dog will have to navigate what can seem like a labyrinth of trees and maze of pathways that all look similar; small woodland creatures will be close enough to see; squirrels and rabbits, and occasionally deer, will catch the attention of your dog. For these reasons, it is always a good idea to leash your dog, even on these trails. The best-case scenario is he goes chasing after one of these little ones, but he could also run across something more aggressive. It could be a skunk, bobcat, coyote, or even a mountain lion. As we encroach on the natural habitats of these animals, they get more comfortable seeing us and get closer than we anticipate.

You are much more likely to encounter an off-leash dog on the trails than you are in the city. Assuming you have yours on a leash for your run, this can present a power dynamic that the dogs can sense almost immediately. When two dogs are unleashed, they have the freedom to come and go as they please, and when they encounter one another, they have full autonomy to approach or avoid. When they are both leashed, it is up to the owners to make the decision and communicate whether introducing the dogs is a good idea or moving along is the best course. The dynamic of a dog off-leash meeting a dog on a leash can be a little strange, if not downright uncomfortable. Just know that even if you have a well-behaved, approachable, laid-back dog, and you let them roam free, you are not always in control of who they try to interact with.

A lot of people who have dogs that do not play nice usually end up using our service. I can get them acquainted and comfortable with their running buddies, but it's always a bit of a wild card when another dog approaches. If they are on a leash, I pull over off the trail and politely decline and move along. If an off-leash dog approaches, my only recourse is to get in front of any and all dogs that may react negatively in the situation and act as a physical barrier until the other party can corral their dog to move along.

Sounds

*   **Urban:** The noise pollution of the city can be harsh. Buses, garbage trucks, and construction sites are all common offenders. As much sound as these vehicles make, it's the rumble of the earth that can be unnerving for a dog. This is more of a reason to keep them close. If your dog has anxiety over this, do your best to avoid the main roads where the street traffic is highest. Busy intersections bring honking and revving engines. Motorcycles and sports cars can also add to the confusion with their high-pitch motors or loud unfiltered mufflers. I think more than the sights, it's the sounds that cause fear and trepidation in dogs. Keeping them on a near leash is your best bet. Being able to soothe them and let your dog know that they have you close will help put them at ease.
*   **Trail:** The sounds are generally soothing. In most instances, I do my best to highlight the merits and give a fair representation of the benefits and setbacks of each setting, but the trail sounds win this one in a landslide. The sounds are the rhythmic plodding of your steps, the birds that occupy the trees, the running of a water source—if there is one—or other dogs barking in the distance.

Smells

*   **Urban:** These can range from disgusting to delicious. Whether it's discarded food that didn't quite make it into the trash can, or any host of other things, your dog's keen sense of smell will

pick it up. I've seen some dogs that are expert-level scoop and scarf artists. Meaning, they have an uncanny ability to snatch something off the ground mid-run and swallow it before you realize what has happened. If it's a greasy cheeseburger or piece of pizza, it may be a non-issue, but if it is a chicken bone, you may run into a larger problem.

The issue with chicken bones in particular is that they can break and the sharp edges could puncture the internal linings of the intestines or get stuck in the throat, causing your dog to choke. If they aren't choking, your first call should be to your veterinarian; give them as many clear details as you can so they can give you a course of action. Do your best to remain calm during the ordeal. You could trigger your dog's alert senses, cause quite the commotion, and inadvertently hurt him/her.

- **Trail:** The scent of potential prey is the most dangerous offender. Especially if your dog is off-leash, it is a candidate to give you the slip and go chasing for a snack that could take it far away from you and out of earshot. Most of the time, the woodlander is too quick or will go up a tree, which will end the chase soon enough. However, if you are near a road and your dog is off-leash, they will give no attention to where they are, the only mission is to seek and destroy; the tunnel vision could cause them to cross into traffic without a second thought, and a fatal outcome could be a real possibility.

Leash

- **Urban:** I always recommend the shortest leash you can comfortably run with so the dog has his space and you have yours. In the city, I specifically recommend using the four-foot Comfort Traffic Leash by KONG® or one similar to it. The ability to get two hands on the leash comfortably in a sudden situation will help keep the dog safer and save you from serious rope burn on your palms. In cities where every inch of space is covered in concrete, taking corners with limited visibility is just a given.

Sarah with Lentil, Cleo, Millie, Gracie, and Harper in Georegtown.

Photo by Chris Roden

I once had a run with an athletic dog who was leashed with a standard collar. I was comfortable with him with that setup because he had demonstrated excellent call-back capacity and never really seemed to want to be much farther from me than his leash allowed. We were on a dirt trail in Rock

Creek Park here in Washington, DC. It's a wonderful park in the center of Northwest DC that is primitive and safe, with a few running trails. Just to our right, and a little behind us, was a bit of wrestling in the near brush. He sensed it, and I gave him a command and pop on the collar to leave it so we could continue with our run. In a weird twist of physics, he simultaneously stopped, pushed back, and shook his head, popping free of the collar. He darted off into the woods, and I just laughed to myself, sort of amused. I was thinking that all I needed to do was call him and he'd return, and no way was he going to catch that squirrel. I called him back, but I may as well have been mute and strapped infrared goggles on him. He was locked in and focused on catching his prey. After calling again with no response, I decided to give chase. The best course of action is to realize that you aren't going to catch the dog, but you need to do your best to keep him in your line of vision, conserving energy when you can because free dogs are sprinters. This all probably lasted ten seconds but, in my mind, it was agonizing. He eventually caught the squirrel and didn't know what to do, and I think he just smothered it out of excitement.

I convey this story, first because I can't believe he actually caught the thing, and second, because you never know what can happen. You can feel helpless at times, even when you're well-trained and comfortable. I was at the mercy of nature in this situation and am thankful the squirrel didn't try to cross the road one hundred yards away.

Being prepared, knowing your dog, and making adjustments after that are how you continue to have successful run outings. I made sure to recommend and use a slip leash in addition to his normal collar for reinforcement. I moved to that tool because he refused to use the Gentle Leader, and we spent more time disagreeing about it. Find the solution that gets the job done and causes the least friction, and you'll both be happy and safer going forward!

Do your best to get in the habit of taking the corners wider to give yourself room to avoid anyone you may not be able to see on the other side. It's difficult enough and strafing can happen when you are simply walking. Now add to the equation that you are on a run, and you have a dog by your side. The last thing you want to do is get tangled with someone who may not share our love of dogs, or even come nose to nose with another dog around the bend. Reaction time is key, and it can mean the difference between pulling back safely and catching some teeth to the ear and nose of your dog.

- **Trail:** Here you can take a little liberty with the leash length because trails generally have better sightlines for potential trouble. But even then, like in the story before, you can be put in a tricky spot. You know your dog well and can make informed decisions, but the case for a shorter leash on trails is that you have fewer opportunities to get caught up in it yourself, have your dog get tangled, have it snag on a rock or root, or even find yourself and your dog splitting a tree and ending up caught in an awkward abrupt stop (assuming you didn't fall or snap them back by the neck).

Understand that even if you follow the leash laws, others may not, and getting upset will only further charge a potentially volatile situation. Do your best to remain calm and put into perspective that this is a five- to ten-second interaction that will pass if you can just ignore them and move forward. If a free dog comes up to your leashed dog on a run, and if they are approaching from the front, you'll get a sense of how your dog is reacting to the attention, and the intentions of the dog coming on. If your dog isn't friendly, spring into action as quickly as possible and put yourself between your dog and the approaching dog. Do your best to use any calming tactics that may help, and walk perpendicular or in the opposite direction. The idea behind this movement is to break the focus and distract your dog from the situation. If you can succeed in this, you have a better chance of redirecting the attention to you and the calmness you are exhibiting. Hopefully, the other party can corral their dog, but even if they don't, do your best to remain calm. Your energy, especially when reactive, can alert your dog, and they could lash out as well. Let them pass and continue on with your day. You're already enjoying a run with your best friend, so let the moment fade, or run the frustration off!

Other Obstacles

- **Urban:** Grates in the sidewalk are a common sight in major cities. You'll know pretty quickly if your dog is wary of them. If so, do your best to keep your eyes on the ground and steer your dog around and away from them. I've been victim to the abrupt stop, only to turn around and see a dog planted inches from a grate because they are unsure if they should run across them. Some dogs have no issues and will run right over them,

Nicole with Scout in Rock Creek Park.

Photo by Chris Roden

while others are unsure, so their survival instinct activates, and they act with self-preservation in mind.

- **Trail:** Ticks. Put this tally in the column of running on a leash and sticking to the trails. Avoiding tall grass, wooded areas, and thick brush will save you heartache and medical bills. Ticks cannot jump, so they rest in these areas and wait for dogs (and humans) to run by and brush up against them. They attach quickly and look for an opportunity to bite. It only takes twenty-four to forty-eight hours for the Lyme Disease they carry to get into your bloodstream. Prevention: Inspect your dog and yourself thoroughly, and if you find one, remove it using tweezers. Research and ask your veterinarian for recommendation on a spray that will be safe for your dog to use. Avoid running off-leash through the woods.

- **Both:** Sharp rocks, sticks, roots, broken glass, and other miscellaneous sharp objects that cover the ground can all cause serious damage to your dog's pads. If cut, burned, ripped, or worse, it could mean a hobbled dog limping all the way back to the car. Depending on how severe the injury, it could take minutes to stop the bleeding, or if deeper, it could take much longer. Use a clean cloth to wipe the area and dress the wound when possible. Consider running with an essentials-only running first aid kit. Some gauze, wipes, and tweezers would be a great spartan version. If you are carrying a backpack, add more from the list provided in the first aid checklist in Chapter 8.

Single vs. Multiple

Stopping

- **Single:** You'll know the power of your dog and how vigilant you'll need to be with regard to stopping. A slow, rhythmic pulling on the leash as you decelerate can be enough to get your point across. Grabbing the leash with two hands when necessary and redirecting the momentum can be helpful, as well.

Remember, it's always easier to slow your dog down the closer they are to you. If you have a free spirit dog that likes to weave back and forth on runs, you'll need to pay special attention that they don't end up running behind you, because in the event you need to stop, the leash could end up laying across the back of your legs. That could end in some serious rope burn on the backs of knees, or worse, cutting your legs out from under you and risking an arm injury when you brace from the fall.

- **Multiple:** The basics are the same, but with one caveat: your goal should be to lower your center of gravity and lean back and away from your dogs. With two dogs running in the same direction, the force is multiplied in that direction. Slowing and eventually stopping will take practice, especially during a run. Getting low and shifting your weight into a squat

Penny and Cappy.

stance will give you a wide base and strength to overcome the momentum moving forward. Using your voice commands in concert with your actions will provide the best results.

Passing Other Packs

- **Single:** Always rely on your instincts as you learn your dog. Depending on how old your dog is, you've likely had hundreds, if not thousands, of encounters with other dogs and dog packs. Trust your gut when you see other dogs and people that get your dog's negative attention. There is likely a reason, and it is not necessary that you understand it, but it is a good idea to listen to it.

  One of the best things you can do as you approach other dogs is make eye contact with the person walking or running with them. If you have a well-behaved dog who plays well with dogs and humans alike, a simple nod or widening of the eyes will be enough to signal that you will pass through without incident. You can't always expect it, but if they look at you, you can get a read on their behavior. If they look flustered or as though they are trying to corral their dog, give them a wide berth as you pass. The communication can begin long before any dogs come nose to nose.

- **Multiple:** Err on the side of caution when running with multiple dogs. It can be easy to think that people would notice you and give you plenty of room just based on the spectacle alone, but I've had enough experience to learn that people defend their space and are not so willing to cede it to you and a few dogs. I would recommend being proactive and understanding that you are the one exercising behavior that is abnormal. Because you are running, others may just be trying to register the sight and they may not even realize that giving you space would help. Avoid congested intersections and sidewalks. Run to areas that are not densely populated and make a habit of pulling over to the side when you pass other dogs and packs. Similar to when

Sarah with Millie, Cleo, and Harper in Georgetown.

Photo by Chris Roden

your dog on a leash encounters one that is off-leash, there is a bit of a power dynamic. When you have multiple dogs, even seemingly well-behaved dogs, they can fall victim to the pack mentality, and all it takes is a small spark from one of your dogs or the approaching one for chaos to erupt. Check your ego, pull over, verbally confirm if your dogs are approachable, and then continue on with the run. Pulling over can mean just giving the other owner more space, or it can mean stopping and getting the attention of your dogs until they pass so you can continue.

Leash Setup

- **Single:** Reference "Chapter 4: Tools for Running" and decide on the least amount of gear you can use to maintain confidence and control of your dog in the event of a negative encounter. Yes, you care about the everyday running and how they react with the setup, but it is important that in those few moments when dogs will be dogs that you have the capability to regain control of the situation. Invest the time and money in figuring this out. I've laid out my thoughts on the particular tools that I find helpful, but talk to your trainer, if you have one, or engage with one on social media. I've answered dozens of questions about running with dogs from families I will never be able to physically serve. I'm always open and happy to talk about specifics on Instagram, Facebook, and Twitter!

- **Multiple:** The goal is to always create a setup for yourself that has you only holding one leash handle. If you are running with two dogs, I would recommend a specialty leash that has one handle but divides into two bolt snaps for leashing two separate dogs. This gives them room to breathe and run in different positions, e.g., one in front and one to the side.

Try out a coupler that attaches to any leash and bifurcates it, turning it into a leash that allows you to strap two in together. These usually keep the dogs closer together during the run but are still effective. There aren't that many households with more than two dogs that are also all capable of running, but for you, I have a solution, as well.

If you don't want to buy any additional gear, there is a solution that will allow you to run them together or apart from one another. When I'm running two dogs and have left my specialty leash or coupler at home, I am still prepared to run multiple dogs safely. I go more in-depth in "Chapter 4: Tools for Running," but want to highlight the merits of my recommendations here, too. Using the Metropolitan Leash, I connect one end to my alpha dog and then subsequently connect my Traffic Leashes to any remaining dogs in the pack. Next, I loop the handles on to the free end of the Metropolitan Leash and bolt-snap it to its nearest D-ring, six inches or so away, creating a single handle that I can hold. The goal is always having one leash in your hand, so any solutions you can create on your own will help you run them safely.

The last and definitely most cost-effective way to solve this is to buy yourself a quality carabiner. These are tools used for climbing that are rugged and capable of handling hundreds of pounds of stress. You can easily clip multiple leashes together with it and run with it or one of the leash handles. The only major drawback of this solution is that because you aren't using the tool as necessarily intended, they can have unintended effects on each other. The carabiner will be fine, but you may find that your leash handles begin to wear because they rub in ways they aren't designed to function. It's sort of like using the butt of a screwdriver as a hammer, you may get some nails in the wood, but that screwdriver won't last as long as it could or should.

Running Style

- **Single:** Anything goes and is fair game! Whatever makes you and your dog comfortable will produce the most fun and best results. Try to find a balance with them that leaves some slack in the line. It's not fun if you have an overeager dog that is leaping out front, weaving across the path, and taking you where his nose takes him. Contrast that with a dog that is running behind on a taut leash, and even if you may not be dragging him along, there will be discomfort in his neck from the collar being pulled on. Adjust your own running pace to match their energy and pace. The primary objective is for you to be comfortable and capable of drawing them near if needed. I don't mind if they run out front to your side or back to one side, wherever you feel comfortable with them running is just fine. I would strongly recommend that if they do run behind, you don't let the leash rest against your leg and work to keep the leash on the same side they are running on. We are trying to avoid him chasing something and taking your legs out with him as he goes.

- **Multiple:** The only major difference here is that I would not let them run behind me. Dogs all have unique thoughts and desires on the run, and sometimes they are in conflict about which way they want to go. Turning your head to check on

David with Lentil and Bear in Washington, DC.

Photo by Chris Roden

them constantly is a hassle, but it's also a safety concern because it takes your eyes off the road ahead. You are also more likely to get tangled up and tripped on leashes if they are near your legs.

Running in an urban setting and trail setting are wildly different and require different solutions to be enjoyable, productive, and safe. Your main concern, as always, should be safety, but knowing your surroundings can help. If you are new to an area, I would suggest only walking as you get to learn that particular setting. Go for a few solo runs, and at different times of day where possible. There are likely congested times of the day that would make it miserable for you and your dog to try and run. After work on a Friday in a trendy spot in town could yield the same negative result as a Memorial Day run on a hike-able trail.

Sarah and Harper running in Georgetown.
Photo by Chris Roden

CHAPTER EIGHT:
Before You Start

Step-by-Step Training Plan

Let's say your dog is a bit "healthier" than you'd like them to be. You've been a bit too liberal with the treats, and they've been avoiding the dog gym because ... well, working out is hard. They've been getting their mid-day walk, but the mornings and evenings are just for the bathroom, and the dog park isn't their jam.

It's not lost on us that not all dogs are in marathon shape or even 5K shape. Well, this plan is a great way to get them from the dog-couch to 5K. As always, start a conversation with your veterinarian and let them know of your intentions for the dog. You can bring them the plan I'm drawing up here and say, "This is something I want to do, do I need to modify it or tailor their meals to help weight loss?"

First, they'll be thrilled that you have a step-by-step plan to get your dog up and running. Then, if they're worth their salt, they'll recommend a unique dog food you can switch to, or help you with portion control if they keep you on their current kibble. Like us, dogs are creatures of habit, and having a plan to stick to will help them with transitioning from a current routine (if there is one) to a new regimen.

What we like to do is introduce a walk/run alternating program where you are increasing the run duration weekly or reducing the walking duration over the same time frame. Remember, we're trying to build habits, and shocking the system by trying too much too soon can lead to poor results. It's better to be cautious and build lasting health than to dive in and get overzealous, potentially causing injury.

Owen with Heidi.

Week 1:

Alternate between 2-minute walks and 2-minute runs.

Total: 16-minute walk | 14-minute run

Keep a moderate to slow pace. We're just introducing the activity, and ideally, they are still getting their other regular walks during the day.

Week 2:

Alternate between 2-minute walks and 3-minute runs.

Total: 12-minute walk | 18-minute run

Again, keep a moderate to slow pace. They'll be a little more used to the activity and may be anxious to run more, but your job is to be the voice of reason and make sure they keep it to the recommended times.

Week 3:

Alternate between 2-minute walks and 4-minute runs.

Total: 10-minute walk | 20-minute run

Stay patient. I know they will be doing much better, but it is better to continue holding them back and building a good base.

Week 4:

Alternate between 2-minute walks and 6-minute runs three times (and a 4-minute run the last time).

Total: 8-minute walk | 22-minute run

We get a little aggressive here and bump up the run by an extra minute while maintaining the two-minute walk breaks. The run ends with a four-minute run for a thirty-minute cap. The idea here is to assess the dog to see if they continue building stamina or if we need to repeat week 3 to continue building endurance.

Week 5:

Alternate between 1-minute walks and 9-minute runs.

Total: 3-minute walk | 27-minute run

Stay patient. I know they will be doing much better while gaining stamina and endurance, but it is beneficial to their habit and health to continue holding them back and building a good base.

Week 6:

Alternate between 12-minute runs and a 6-minute walk.

Total: 6-minute walk | 24-minute run

Phillip with Bear.

Even though the totals stay the same from week 5 to week 6, the added duration to the run portion will build cardiovascular strength. All other weeks begin on a walk, but this week, do not begin timing until the first run interval begins. There is only one six-minute break right in the middle of the exercise. You are taxing their system this week on both ends with extended runs, so use the break to offer water, check for non-verbal communication, and see if your dog is up for continuing the run. If modifications need to be made, do so on the back half of the run and mix in an extra walk segment. You can also choose to step back and repeat week 5.

After week 6, it is up to you to continually assess your dog's progress, while continuing to monitor his safety. Stretch out the running segment until you have a dog that can go a full thirty minutes without needing a break. Also, adjust the pace accordingly as the run durations increase. Slow the pace down and continue to work on good habits and form, and as you both get stronger, you will soon realize that it is probably you who's holding the dog back!

Once you and your dog can run for thirty minutes uninterrupted, you can begin to test the limits of his capabilities. Re-evaluating him after these runs will tell you if he is comfortable to continue adding an extra mile or if he has topped out. Monitoring his recovery time is just as important as his status during the run. If you go for seven miles and see signs of soreness with slow movement, hold that distance for the time being. It is expected that he/she be tired the remainder of the day and maybe even the next, but if it that continues any further, stay at that distance and consider reducing the distance. If near the end of the run he is maintaining the pace you have set and doesn't look overworked, continue on. Building the strength and stamina over time will allow you and your dog to add miles to your runs.

The story of Ludivine, the dog who accidentally ran a half marathon, is fantastic! It was race day in Elkmont, Alabama, and people were taking part in the Trackless Train Trek Half Marathon. At her home near the start line, April Hamlin let her dog, Ludivine, out to do her business. Ludivine saw the commotion and snuck under her fence and joined in the race. She stayed mostly with the lead runners, but chased a rodent off course at least once. A total of 13.1 miles later she had finished the race in seventh place! She earned a medal and everything. The organizers of the race were so taken with her, they subsequently renamed the race: The Hound Dog Half. It has a medal with her likeness on it and has helped them raise money for the local high school cross country team.

There are others who have ventured even farther; *Runner's World* magazine profiled three such dogs in 2014. Colt, a black Labrador, was accustomed to ten-mile runs with his owner, but had the ability to bump up to twenty-five in the best conditions—where a stream or snow was available and the temperatures were cool. Super Bee, a Border Collie, was known to pace her ultra-runner owner as far as thirty-one miles and would regularly run ninety miles a week to help with training. Ben, a German Shorthaired Pointer, trained with his owner and completed one-hundred-mile weeks and peaked at forty miles in one day!

The limits of these exceptional dogs are incredible and highlight the upper reaches of what these special animals are capable of doing. The first dog, Ludivine, without training or any notice, picked up and completed a half marathon. The latter three dogs all had serious training partners who kept track of their own mileage, meaning they had specific training to extend the distance in a safe way. A common theme was the runners all mentioned the exuberance and joy these particular dogs had for running.

First Aid Kits

A search on the internet for a proper first aid kit for dogs will yield page after page of suggestions. What I will offer here is a spartan version you can carry with you in your backpack if you decide to head off on a long run in a more remote setting where field dressing is your best option. Ideally, all of this can be kept in a resealable plastic bag or something similar in size.

First Aid Kit for Dogs

- **Tools:** Tweezers are small but versatile in that they can help you remove splinters, thorns, and stickers from their pads and body. Sometimes fingernails are not enough to extract a foreign object quickly to help your canine. A small bottle of saline solution will help you clean the wound site initially. Use antibiotic ointment to help you clean the wound and prevent infection. Cotton balls or swabs will help you wipe away blood or debris from a wound site and also help apply the antibiotic ointment without the danger of spreading germs into the wound. A gauze roll is helpful to the protect the wound site after it has been cleaned. Bandage tape will keep the gauze in place.

- **Medication:** Hydrogen peroxide is handy in the event that your dog ingests something poisonous and you need to induce vomiting. It is best to write instructions on the bottle after speaking

Bryan with Molly on the Capital Crescent Trail in Washington, DC.

with your veterinarian. The likelihood is that you need to act fast, so having the information available and quickly will save time and ensure you deliver the appropriate amount. Having Benadryl will help bring down the swelling in the event your dog has an allergic reaction to a wasp/bee sting. The important piece of information when searching for Benadryl is to get one that only has diphenhydramine as the active ingredient and not a combo cold/flu type.

Anything beyond these essentials, and you'll need to think about substituting for space. If the list grows any longer, the kit will grow larger and you will be less likely to carry it with you on runs. The important thing is having essentials available to you to cover for the situations you are most likely to find yourself in.

Other Dog Runners

Dog running has become increasingly popular as a profession, definitely since I began running seven years ago. With that comes a wealth of knowledge to tap into from others who own dog-running companies. I enlisted the help of some dog runners from around the country who range from new on the job to over a decade in the field. In talking with them, I found they had unique experiences that were helpful, and I wanted to share them with you, too! I think it will help you in realizing that just like no two dogs are alike in running style, dog runners have different solutions that help them run with dogs safely and confidently.

I interviewed:

David Hill — Canine Pacers in Denver, Colorado

Alyxe Roberts — Furry Fit in Orange County, California

Clayton Roth — Canine Cardio Rhode Island in Providence, Rhode Island

Jordan Ryan — Ruff Runners in Atlanta, Georgia

Willie Bogue — Hightail Dog in Portland, Oregon

Birdie lounging in her yard.

I felt like these runners and companies covered all corners and climates the United States has to offer. They experience different seasons and offer valuable insights into challenges for dog runners that I may not have encountered personally. It also adds value to you the reader, because while I do have experiences and offer solutions, it is always great to collaborate with others who have a different perspective.

Q: What is one piece of gear or equipment that is indispensable?

David Hill of Canine Pacers says, "Freedom Harness. There are quite a few good harnesses out there, but that's the one I always gravitate back to using. Using the front chest clip on the harness is quite effective at discouraging pulling. And of course, I'm biased, but the Canine Ice Vest during the summer."

David has operated a dog-running company for nearly thirteen years and is the inspiration to me starting my own dog-running company. His company in Chicago was profiled by *Runner's World* magazine and he was generous with his time when speaking with me about the trials, tribulations, and joys of launching a dog-running company. He is also the inventor of the Canine Ice Vest I recommended in "Chapter Six: Seasonal Solutions."

Alyxe Roberts of Furry and Fit says, "A running belt. This is a lifesaver. I am able to run hands-free with certain packs by clipping the leashes to my belt. I am able to carry a water bottle, phone, business cards, keys, and doggie bags very easily. I used to run with a smaller belt, but it didn't hold as much, and when I'm running on more remote trails, I feel most comfortable carrying my phone in case something were to happen to me or the dogs."

Alyxe learned her craft and found her calling as a dog runner working with DC Dog Runner while in college.

Jordan Ryan of Ruff Runners says, "Waist-locking leash. Using this type of leash ensures that the dog is attached to the runner at all times, which provides security should a runner trip or if a dog tries to run after a squirrel."

Other runners also cited hands-free leashes. While it isn't my go-to, it definitely aligns with my thinking that having at least one hand free is vital while running, and having two provides benefits, as well. As long as the equipment allows you to perform the activity safely and confidently, I support it!

Q: Are there any challenges to dog running that you see that are unique to your city?

Clayton Roth of Canine Cardio Rhode Island says, "I am fairly certain that Driver's Ed instructors skip the turn signal section here in New England. Drivers just don't use them, and it can be quite hairy when running in and around Providence. I am not a mind reader, please use your turn signal! It almost seems like there is a control center designed to make runs in the city difficult."

Heidi, Beckett, Bear, Maximus, and Huxley on the lawn of the Saint John Paul II National Shrine.

On a phone call, Clayton also highlighted that residential neighborhoods were dangerous, as well, due to drivers not being focused when backing out of driveways, or being distracted by texting, or in a hurry and not being aware of their surroundings.

Willie Bogue of Hightail Dog says, "The legendary rain in Portland can sometimes last for weeks without relenting. Also, any amount of snow completely immobilizes the city, which can make getting to and from clients' homes challenging. And wet, cold, running gloves can make for numb fingers, which isn't fun."

This highlights factors that are out of your control for running. The local response to inclement weather can make things tough for you. Portland is accustomed to the showers and how to negotiate the problems that arise, but snow occurs infrequently and can cause difficulties.

David Hill says, "Rattlesnakes are an issue if you go to trails outside Denver around sunrise or dusk. Denver gets a healthy dose of all four seasons, so managing the hottest and coldest days are the main challenge."

Understanding your area is exposed to both the heat of the summer and cold of the winter will help you in acquiring the specific tools that can help you year round. It might also be helpful to use a tool or gear box to keep the equipment that may only be used for part of the year.

Q: What is the largest number of dogs you've run with at once? Would you run with more? When does it become unsafe?

Alyxe Roberts says, "The most I've run with is four dogs. I would run more if I knew them all individually and knew they were well-trained, controllable, and a like-minded pack. It becomes unsafe with as little as two dogs if the pair doesn't work well together."

When building a pack for running, it is important that you establish a relationship with each dog individually before introducing them to each other. Gaining their trust by exhibiting confidence is important. (Refer to "Chapter 2: Assessing Your Dog for the First Time" for more information on this.) To lead the pack you need to learn to lead each dog or there will likely be unrest and behavioral problems from those who don't know whether to follow you or another dog in the pack.

David Hill says, "Once on the Chicago lakefront I ran six dogs together, all I knew quite well. The largest regular run I've done is four dogs at once. My staff runs no more than three at one time. I would say, even with years of experience, running more than four dogs becomes risky and potentially unsafe."

What stood out about this response was that even though there is the ability to run more, there is a point where doing something wise and safely often is the best approach. Your knowledge and relationships with the dogs will continue to surface as qualifying factors for these answers.

Willie Bogue says, "I've only ever run with one at a time, though I'd be willing to run with a second dog from the same household. For me, two is the max. I wouldn't be able to keep a handle on any more than that."

This highlights that while some may feel comfortable with multiple dogs, sometimes running with a single dog is more than enough. Know your limits and enjoy your run!

Jordan Ryan says, "We currently max out at two, and are unlikely to run more together unless the circumstances are unique. The more

Bryan with Scout and company trail running.

dogs you add the more risk there is that the runner or another dog could get hurt, and with the number of distractions along the Atlanta city streets, keeping the numbers low is ideal."

Jordan runs most of his miles in an urban setting, so fewer dogs for packs makes sense when the sidewalks are narrow and pedestrians and cars are a constant.

Q: What is the most difficult season to run? What makes it so tough? How do you overcome the elements?

Clayton Roth says, "Winter. I grew up in Northern Michigan. Lots of snow. We don't get that much fluffy stuff here in Rhode Island, but when we do, it makes getting around quite difficult. As in most urban areas, there's just nowhere to put snow after a storm. It piles up, taking parking spots and covering sidewalks we might use for our walks and runs. Warm gear goes without saying, but Yaktrax®, or an equivalent, are great for snowy or icy conditions."

Jordan Ryan says, "Summer. The heat and humidity make it very difficult for dogs to efficiently cool their bodies, but their body and mind want the exercise. Getting a lot of energy out without overworking a dog can be both difficult and dangerous if not done safely. We try to reschedule runs to the cooler parts of the day, but it isn't always possible. Assuming the weather isn't extreme, we remind parents to keep their dogs hydrated at home, and we provide water along the run. We run in the shade as much as possible, take breaks often, and cool dogs down by pouring water on their neck/back (evaporating water will take heat with it)."

Willie Bogue says, "Winter. If it's raining, I'm bound to get soaked no matter what, so I don't bother with rain jackets. I just bring a couple changes of shoes and socks in the car. We rarely get days so hot that the pavement is dangerous to use dog pads, but when we do, clients are usually amenable to an early morning run instead of their usual time."

Beckett, Wookie, and Rocco adding their own fragrance to the car.

David Hill says, "Summer. Making sure the dogs don't get too hot and experience heat stroke. I try to run earlier in the day. Most of our runs with dogs are finished by noon or 1 p.m. We use a cooling garment that helps mitigate rising core body temperature in dogs quite well. We also stop to give the dogs water and take short rest breaks in the shade on the warmer days."

Alyxe Roberts says, "Summer. The temperatures aren't too hot compared to east coast summers, but the sun is extremely strong and there is no shade. I live on the coast and most days it doesn't get over 80 degrees. Just looking at those temperatures one would think it would be perfect for running any time of day. Unfortunately, because there aren't many big trees and the dirt is so dry, it heats up so quickly. I have adjusted by starting runs as early as 7:45 a.m. and as late as 6 p.m. Clients are very understanding, and it has worked out well so far. Adjusting the time of day we run, find new trails that are shaded at certain times of the day, run on grass fields, and bring water."

Learning from the experience of others is a great resource at our disposal. Accepting that there are multiple ways to solve a problem and searching for a better solution can make you a better dog runner. Also, having a plan of action for your journey to begin running will ensure you build the strength, stamina, and habit of running.

Sarah, Cleo, and JFK.

Photo by Chris Roden

Gwynne and Oskar running along the Lincoln Memorial Reflecting Pool.

Photo by Chris Roden

CHAPTER NINE:
Types of Running Dogs

Having heard from different runners across the country, it only seemed fair to highlight some of the dogs we run! These are the dog breeds we are commonly asked to work with and have gained valuable insight into. They could be a good fit for runners who are considering getting a dog. I'll also add that even within dog breeds, each dog has his own desire and willingness to run for exercise. Because of that fact, finding a way to comprehensively talk about mixed-breed dogs seemed too wide of a scope to package neatly in a section below. There are no absolutes with dog running, so spending time with your dog and assessing them ("Chapter Two: Assessing Your Dog for the First Time") or having someone else do it ("Chapter Ten: Finding & Working with a Dog Runner"), will help you along the way.

Portuguese Water Dog

Type of Runner
These dogs are durable, consistent daily runners. They have a fantastic build and energy level that makes them great for both city and

trail runs. They fare better in cooler temperatures for longer runs and are happy to keep a moderate pace with bursts of energy when they come across something they love.

Their top-end speed isn't the highest, so elite runners who run long distances at a quicker pace may not be the best fit. They've got an upright look about them while running that can only be described as regal. Maybe that's why the former president had two!

They are not competitive runners. This means that in packs, they do not have a preference for being upfront and leading, and they have no issues letting other dogs (or humans) push the pace. As I mentioned earlier, they are not top-end speedsters, but they are deceptively athletic. Their typical curly fur can make them look a little bulky and are actually prone to weight gain if not exercised daily. In addition to weight gain, they have a tendency to be destructive when they fall short of their needed physical stimulation.

Best suited for: Long, steady runs | Trails with obstacles

About

They are called "Portie" for short because Portuguese Water Dogs can be sort of a mouthful. These dogs are highly intelligent, loving, and loyal. They are naturals in the water, but how could they not be with "water" in their name?

If you are active and live near a body of water or own a pool, this breed is probably what you have been searching for. Same goes for families that love to be on a boat. These dogs are typically fun-loving, smart, and eager to please. It's because of these characteristics that they can also be easy to train, but be aware that because they are prone to becoming overweight, using treats can be tricky.

Originally from the Portuguese coast, they made their way to Newfoundland by working the boats with fishermen. They are considered the herding dogs of the water. Rather than wrangling livestock and sheep, they would help steer the fish toward nets for the fishermen. Other jobs on the boat for the Portie included retrieving

Cappy at his home in Nantucket, Massachusetts.

equipment that may have fallen overboard and acting as messengers to send notes back and forth between boats.

My Experience

I've run with a couple of Porties, and all of my best stories come from Captain. He is roughly ten now and has aged out of running daily, but at one point, he had the stamina and build to go for daily thirty-minute runs with me. We ran with him for two and a half years, and he was a good companion to keep you alert! He grew up in a three-Portie home and was six and ten years younger than his older sister and brother, respectively.

When I met him, he was a bit too rambunctious for his sister (and owner). He needed a little more attention than the walks he was getting, and he was protective of his home and those in it. Gaining his trust was necessary, but once you had it, you were his. One of the things we used running to solve for was his over-aggressiveness toward dogs he perceived as a threat. Sometimes getting him out the door was a chore, and he'd make me come to him to affix his Gentle Leader, but once out, he was a consistent runner that gave great effort and was excited to be out.

In our time together, he was able to help me give a good test to potential runners we were considering hiring. The thinking being: it is paramount that you be alert during the run, and Cappy especially required focus to avoid conflict. He definitely taught me to be considerate of blind corners on runs with dogs and redirect his attention, or pre-emptively soothe it, as another dog or pack of dogs approached. His instinct was to bark loudly and lunge at almost any dog he encountered, but we learned that patience is the key to forming strong relationships. With any new dogs I introduced him to, I made sure to give them distance and time to realize the threat was nonexistent, a practice I still use to this day anytime I'm introducing new dogs to one another.

Weimaraner

Type of Runner

All-purpose. These dogs are incredible running partners. They are definitely in the top five all-around running dogs in my opinion. They like to get out front, especially when they are in a pack. They are big impressive runners that command presence and need an alert runner. You'll need to be confident and strong in your movement with them. If they smell something interesting, they'll want to follow it or stop to investigate. You'll need to be ready to keep them focused. They are built for long, fast runs with their short hair, big chest for lung capacity, long legs, and lean, but muscular, bodies. The only drawback is that they can overpower a small or inexperienced runner with their movements. If you aren't proactive on the run, meaning on the lookout for distractions, and redirecting their attention, they can pull you off course. They have an effortless gait that can make you feel as if you aren't moving particularly fast, but that is just because they are efficient with their stride. They can be a little territorial of their home and owner, so, again, staying vigilant is a must. They can do speed work with you for fartlek runs, go long distances if trained up, are agile and athletic if you like single-track trail runs, and really seem to enjoy churning out miles. They'll need pretty consistent attention in terms of running—four to five days a week of thirty minutes to an hour should be the expectation. Going to the park is great, and throwing and chasing are all well and good, but these guys want to get out and on with it. This dog should be at the top of any runner's list, especially if you have experience with running dogs.

Megan and Maximus.

Photo by Chris Roden

Best suited for: Long, steady runs | Going fast | Running on trails

About

Known as the "Silver Ghost" or "Grey Ghost," these German dogs have become popular for their striking coat and piercing eyes. They are hunting dogs that handle big game like bear and deer. As noted above, they require constant attention and exercise. They are intelligent dogs and are highly trainable. Weimaraners can appear intimidating but are generally friendly dogs that do well with active families.

Weimaraners became popular in the United States during the 1950s due to celebrity owners President Dwight D. Eisenhower and movie star Grace Kelly. This passage from the Weimaraner Club of America is telling: "Weimaraners are the perpetual two-year-old—loveable, active, loyal to a fault, and with the attitude, 'It's all about ME!'" While I love them, I have to utter the time-worn phrase, "They're not a breed for everyone."

My Experience

I've run with a few Weimaraners, and two that stick out are Captain and Maximus. Captain is a racer; no matter how many in the group, he wants to physically lead the pack. He doesn't much care for or notice the other pack members and is hardly an alpha, but when it comes to running, he wants to be first. I first noticed it when we held a group run. Anytime another runner and dog moved ahead of us he would begin to pull on the leash. I assumed he just wanted to interact with the other dog, but he would run past them and then would ease off the gas a bit. He is incredibly athletic, and I've yet to outrun him. With Maximus, we've learned that he is a true escape artist. He has slipped his crate a few times and knows when he has a little freedom. However, he is trained very well and listens to and follows commands. He goes on long runs with his owners, and our team has filled in to supplement his miles! Both males are large and require strength and confidence to run. I've consistently ranked Weimaraners in the top five all-purpose running dogs.

Border Collie

Type of Runner

Above average for distance, superb agility, smart, and calm. A great companion for tight trails or rolling hills. This is a working-class dog that can keep a great upbeat pace for longer distances but also excels at short bursts of speed while staying under control. They fare much better in the fall, winter, and early spring due to their long hair, but the drop-off in the summer isn't noticeable if you cut them short and keep them on trails under the shade. Because of their herding ability, they are experts at staying on balance and being able to navigate turns on a winding, narrow trail. In the wide-open space, they are patient runners who are most happy when they have their own space. If trained well, they can help you break new dogs into running by keeping them focused and on task.

Ellie on a sunny day in Chevy Chase, Maryland.

Best suited for: Long, steady runs | Running in the cold

About

The "Border" in Border Collie comes from the region they are from, the border of Scotland and England. The word "Collie" refers to sheepdogs and is derived from a Scottish dialect. They are elite herding dogs and primarily work with sheep. Border Collies are highly trainable due to their intelligence and they have energy, stamina, and a great working drive. Their exercise needs are, overall, high, but with a need to stay active rather than have short bursts to tire them out.

A natural outlet for Collies is herding classes or agility training. They are nimble and balanced runners who maintain body control and have excellent reaction time and reflexes. The popular website Dogtime.com has this to say about the breed: "This breed likes to be busy. In fact, he must be busy or he becomes bored, which leads to annoying behavior, such as barking, digging, or chasing cars. He's not a dog to lie quietly on the front porch while you sip a glass of lemonade; he thrives on activity."

My Experience

The female (Ellie) that I've run with is a light-footed smaller Border Collie who loves her own space. On solo runs, she's a perfect companion and runs right by my side with slack in the line and follows my direction with the slightest nudge of the lead in the direction we need to go. On pack runs she is happy to lay back while the others jockey for position out front. She'll happily stay a step behind me and never pushes nor drags the pace.

The male (Rocco), or Franken-Collie, is our longest-tenured runner. He is such a happy runner and is more vocal than his female counterpart. He's friendly, but likes to push the pace a little more with his housemates and neighbors, but never pulls. He's an incredibly capable runner that has stamina and burst when needed. A well-trained Border Collie is a dream running partner to train with for a middle-distance race.

Mala on a paved trail in Washington, DC.

Rhodesian Ridgeback

Type of Runner

These beautiful dogs are confident, strong-minded runners who cannot be hurried. They are incredibly capable and gifted long-distance runners. They run efficiently and know how to conserve energy. Hot days don't bother these short-haired dogs who originated in Africa. They are efficient runners and can keep up despite looking a bit disinterested. The males specifically are large and do best with a strong, capable runner who can be firm and in control. They seem to put their running on autopilot and will maintain a steady pace and can hold it for miles! These are great running companions for midpackers who may run miles in the dark early in the morning or after they get home. They are fearless and will protect you.

Best suited for: Running in the heat | Long, steady runs

About

The Rhodesian Ridgeback breed was established in 1922 and is called "African Lion Hound." These dogs are known for being loyal, mild-tempered, yet brave. They are one part domesticated wild dog and part European imports (Great Danes, Mastiffs, Greyhounds, Bloodhounds). Hunters were looking for a dog that could help on hunts as well as guard the homestead. The breeders noticed that the crosses who had ridges on their backs were excellent hunters.

They are identifiable by the hair pattern that grows in the opposite direction along the spine. They have short hair and perform much better in warmer temperatures than cooler ones. They have above-average intelligence but a stubborn will, so training them can be challenging. Because of their history of protecting, they get along well and are affectionate with their family, but are standoffish with strangers.

My Experience

We've run with eight or so Ridgebacks. They've almost all been very strong-willed. It takes a certain demeanor to own and run with a Rhodesian Ridgeback. Running with these dogs can be difficult for those new to dog running. They can be stubborn and are best suited to running with a confident, strong (both physically and mentally) runner. You don't need to be a disciplinarian, but you cannot be a doormat. It takes patience and forgiveness to find a pace and style that works for both of you. I've seen it all; one dog refused to go in the SUV with me. Another wanted to sprint as soon as we got out the door. You can harness that energy and power to slow them down, but I can't think of a single occasion where I was able to speed them up. Understanding that the best run isn't always the fastest will lead to longer-lasting, better results.

Vizsla

Type of Runner

All-purpose. This dog would be the decathlete of the Olympics. They would run a respectable 100 meters but would shine in the middle and long distances. Their bodies are built for an easy stride to cover a lot of ground quickly. Their long legs ensure that they won't be left behind, while a sturdy body gives them the strength and endurance to run long. They are a fantastic combination of speed and power. They have enough of both to keep up with ultra-marathoners who push the limits like Michael Wardian and his dog, Rosie. Vizslas are svelte, efficient runners who make it look effortless. They also aren't so big as to give smaller runners fits on a leash. They're great on the roads and equally agile and nimble on single-track trails that can sometimes narrow to the point of disappearing. If your plan includes going long and fast, the Vizsla may be for you. They are best suited for a family that has a runner in it because they need to get out daily for at least thirty minutes, and longer if possible.

Best suited for: Long, steady runs | Going fast | Running on trails | Running in the heat

Ollie

About

AKC.org says of the Vizsla, "As a hunter expected to work closely with humans, Vizslas form a tight bond with their owners and hate to be left alone." Vizslas are social dogs that crave attention and like to be stimulated mentally and physically. They work hard and are incredibly affectionate at home. They are originally from Hungary, medium in size, and have a solid golden rust-colored coat. They are high energy, but well-mannered unless you are giving attention to another dog. Even on pack runs they like to stay close when on leash and will jockey for position.

Their ancestors were bred to keep up with horses so they selected those that showed an aptitude for keeping up on long, fast-paced journeys. Those traits are ever present today and are a long-distance runner's dream. They do have a tendency to howl and bark, so keeping them in the city where walls are shared may not be the best fit for them. Like most hunting dogs, they are intelligent and easy to train. They have short hair, so grooming is simple and shedding is low.

They are extremely athletic and versatile runners. In a *Runner's World* article I said, "I'd say pound for pound the best running dogs for any type of running. They are so versatile; they can cover a ton of ground because of their long gait and can cruise on autopilot as long as you want." The last thing I'll say before moving on is that if I were going to choose a four-legged running partner to train with me for my next marathon, it would be the Vizsla.

My Experience

We run with a fabulous Vizsla named Ollie. He's a bit tall for the breed but has the stamina to effortlessly pass the miles. He loves attention but has a calm demeanor on the run. He's no fuss and will stick close to you and is happy to go at the pace you set, whether it be slow and long or more active on the dirt trails common in the Washington, DC, area. He's a wonderful hill partner if you need a little assistance going up! He also has a funny quirk of getting silly when the dirt beneath his pads turns to sand. He'll spin in place and get very playful.

Ollie is a sweetheart with the memory of an elephant. We ran for miles and miles without incident, and we would pass by oncoming runners without having to break stride. Then, out of the blue, he went berserk when a dog passed us. It was so out of character, I asked his owners, Rick and Alexis, if anything had set him off that day or during the week, but nothing out of the ordinary had occurred. It happened again a few months later and the lightbulb in my head went off. Both times, he had become incensed by a Rhodesian Ridgeback. I took that information to his owners again, and they confirmed that when he was younger, he had a run-in with a Rhodesian Ridgeback! It seems Ollie never forgot the tussle and held it against every Rhodesian Ridgeback in perpetuity.

German Shorthaired Pointer

Type of Runner

These dogs are strong and confident runners that are most comfortable running in front of a solo runner but at the head of a pack. They like their space, and if not trained properly will pull you along for the ride. For this reason they are popular with Canicross athletes because they assist the runners in navigating trail races where climbing mountains is typical. In this setting the GSP can shine because they are allowed to follow their natural instinct, which is to run hard and fast. Like the Vizsla and Weimaraner, they are strong, durable, with good muscle tone and above-average speed. They are best paired with a confident runner who will let them follow their instincts or a disciplined runner that has time to train them to run by their side. I would recommend this dog as a companion to a seasoned runner who wants to train for long-distance races.

Best suited for: Long, steady runs | Going fast | Running on trails

About

These dogs are medium-sized, athletic, and muscular. They are primarily hunting dogs, and with pointer in the name, it makes sense. They are good at helping locate birds that have been shot during the hunt by pointing their nose and bodies at the game.

They are smart and easier than most to train. They are affectionate and do well with active families who can give them attention. They require lots of exercise and are one of the few that would benefit from running daily. They have short hair, making them easy to groom, and because of this, they handle the hot weather better than the cold.

Originally bread by German hunters, many GSPs were sent to Yugoslavia during World War II, and the breed had to be rebuilt from a limited gene pool in Germany. In the United States they began to show well in field competitions during the late 1960s.

My Experience

One of the first dogs I ever ran with in Dallas was a GSP named Gus. We would run two times a week, and he gave me all I could handle in the beginning! At the time, I was a fairly confident in my ability and assumed running with a standard leash and collar would be the typical setup for all of my dogs. Every run with Gus was the same; it was a struggle for leadership of the run with me holding him back with inadequate tools and stopping to get his attention in an effort to get him to listen to me. The first fifteen minutes were real work and we didn't run much, and then we'd find a groove over the final fifteen at a quick pace. I eventually bumped him up to an hour run and that seemed to help. He was a wonderful dog who just didn't know what to do with his pent-up energy and needed to add a third run to the week.

Bella is a wonderful runner who definitely prefers to run alone. Even when she runs in a pack, it's best if I pick her up first because if there are dogs already in the car, she really hesitates to hop in. This is actually an

Bryan and Gus at Gus's home in Plano, Texas.

improvement from when we first began running. She was very put out by other dogs and would bark to let them know her presence. The great news is she's always been a good listener and put her trust in me. I don't know that I've heard her bark at another dog in over a year, and she enjoys group runs. She's a very happy dog and remains patient. She has sneaky speed and excellent endurance. She runs three times a week and can always keep pace, so long as she uses the bathroom before we begin. If not, she'll throw the breaks on mid-run and go where she's standing! She has also become a great calming influence for Louie (Labrador), and the two of them run most of their miles together.

Australian Shepherd

Type of Runner
Aussies are sure-footed, well-balanced, and agile runners. They are low to the ground and described as being "slightly longer than tall."

This is a perfect description. They are very athletic and can change direction in an instant. They are quick runners that can navigate narrow trails as well or better than most breeds. They can seem distractible, but they just get a bit bored on the run and will look back to you and want to circle around and herd you. They like to be out front and are capable of training for longer distances but do best in the medium distances around ten kilometers.

These dogs are a great fit for everyone, honestly. They have enough stamina to run moderate to long distances but not enough strength to pull you over. They are a great fit if you have a teenager that is a runner or if you have a smaller build. They can also handle year-round weather, and their performance does not fall off that much in the warmer weather.

Best suited for: Trails with obstacles | Year-round running

About

Australian Shepherds are smart dogs who are friendly and affectionate. They are a shepherd, so they definitely possess a strong herding mentality. Aussies have a distinct color known as blue or black merle. While their coats are thick, they perform well during both the colder and warmer months. They are excellent in snow because of their balance and low center of gravity. Like most on this list, their exercise needs and trainability are high—they need to stay active because they have the potential for weight gain.

It may be surprising, but the Aussie is actually an American-born breed. They are Collie and Shepherd mixes bred to help ranchers in the western United States heard livestock. They are closely associated with cowboy culture because of this, and are known to work as rodeo performers!

My Experience

I've run with two Aussies and had remarkably similar experiences with both. In talking about Tahoe, I was quoted in a *Runner's World* article, "The one I run with is the quickest, most agile, sure-footed runner I have in my stable of runners." She was an incredible running companion and excitable and energetic on all the runs. She loved running so much, part of my visit became ensuring she didn't bolt out the door when I arrived. Luckily, she never escaped, but that did not stop her from trying.

Neville joined our pack running with his older sister, Ellie (Border Collie). He was excitable and lovable but in the beginning was more interested in playing around than staying on task for a run. Eventually he learned the routine and became a fantastic running buddy.

A great point about Aussies that I try to share is that they are a great running companion for almost everyone. Their size and temperament fit well with smaller and even younger runners. I was able to pair one up with my young son who joined for a weekend "fun run," where we mostly hiked trails but would trot a little here and there.

Neville posing in front of his Chevy Chase, Maryland, home.

German Shepherd

Type of Runner

These dogs have a strong, work-like approach to running. They have enough speed in short bursts to do sprint work but like to cruise slow and long. They have a very easy, efficient running style and do not fuss. The real treat is that, being highly trainable, they will stick right next to you on any kind of run in any type of condition. They are fantastic city runners for this reason but also excel on trails. They are better suited to cooler weather, so adjusting your runs during the summer or finding shade for them would be wise. Running with them is almost effortless because they are never in competition with you or others in the pack for the lead.

They are best paired with a person who has average to above-average speed that likes to sign up for the occasional 10K or half marathon. They are one of the dogs that do best when they have daily exercise; it doesn't always have to be a long run, but going out for a few miles each day would serve them well.

Best suited for: Running in the cold | Long, steady runs

About

German Shepherds are a very popular dog and are known for their intelligence, loyalty, and work capacity. They are also heralded for their service work with the handicap and their work with police and military units.

Of the 195 breeds the American Kennel Club ranks, the German Shepherd comes in second! It is no surprise, because they are friendly and great with families that have outdoor space and time to spend being active. They need to be physically and mentally stimulated, so running is a natural fit for them.

The famous Rin Tin Tin movies led to the breed becoming popular in the early twentieth century in the United States. However, they fell out of favor during and after World War II. Originally, Captain Max von Stephanitz, a German cavalry officer, developed

German Shepherds to herd livestock. He spent his life advocating for them and eventually began promoting them as K-9 workers. It was because of this devotion they are closely associated with military and police units.

My Experience

Every experience, positive or negative, with the German Shepherd breed is a direct reflection of their training and home life. If the family is calm and laid back, the dog is confident and happy. If the family is exacting and attentive, the dog is alert and active. I've run with a service dog named Koda, an active and curious runner named Arya. The females are a bit more sleek and nimble, while the males definitely command attention and have a presence that requires you to have confidence as a runner.

Like my children, I don't have favorites, but I love running with Heidi! It's actually as close to running solo as I have experienced while dog running. She never pulls and is happy at any pace and for any distance. If you are proactive with GSDs, you can root out the

Heidi is a patient dog!

rodents they may want to chase. As long as I get her attention before she sees them, she'll stay on task and run right next to me. She is a quiet runner, both in that she rarely barks but also her steps are light. I not-so-secretly think she's an undercover detective.

Labrador Retriever

Type of Runner

They are spirited runners that like to tag along but require attention if you are going to run longer than three miles. They are best suited to running slow and shorter distances with breaks for water and shade, especially in the summer. They are one of the few dogs that look like they are working as much as you on the run!

They love pack running and are known to get a little rowdy when they see other dogs passing in the opposite direction. These guys are social by nature, so if you aren't too concerned with how many miles and how fast you are running, they would be a fantastic companion.

Louie taking in the incredible woods near her home in Washington, DC.

Letting them pull over and meet another dog on the trail is easy because of everyone's familiarity with the breed. This can be a drawback if you are an elite runner or want to really push the limits of time and distance. They are great for short runs over hills or sprint work because they'll need the same amount of time as you to recoup, so you won't feel bad about your dog not getting enough exercise.

Be aware that because of their exuberance, they aren't always task-oriented on the runs and tend to veer and drift a bit around you as they run. They enjoy stopping and smelling the roses and may need to be encouraged to finish the run without distraction.

Best suited for: Brisk, short runs | Long, slow runs

About

They are the most popular dog according to the American Kennel Club. Much of that is due to their temperament and disposition; they are friendly, active, and outgoing. They get along well with people and dogs alike. However, they were almost extinct in the late nineteenth century, but the Malmesbury family is given the credit for saving them. They have held the number one position since 1991!

While friendly, they are not laid back and require lots of physical and mental stimulation. Labradors are smart, making them highly trainable, and they are affectionate with small children, strangers, and other dogs. They are comfortable in and around water and love a good swim.

It is helpful to distinguish the American vs. the English Labrador. The American version has a more athletic build with a narrower head whereas his English counterpart is a bit shorter in height and length but stands a bit wider with a boxier head. The English Labrador also has a more laidback demeanor with much less drive to run, especially long distances.

My Experience

I have run with more Labradors than any other breed. It is amazing the variance in the standard for what constitutes a Lab. Factoring out the Labrador mixes (of which there are many), I think they are a good breed for running who have great athleticism but are better suited to the shorter three-mile runs. Louie was specially trained to help as a service animal for persons with seizures. She is incredibly smart and capable but has anxiety herself, and the decision was made that her best fit would be with a family as opposed to serving others. What she found was a fantastic home with young children that love and dote on her and are understanding of her aversions to some activities. They found our service, and we've done our part to help her with socializing and gaining confidence, especially in chaotic and noisy environments. Louie has made incredible strides because she's been put in situations to succeed, like spending time with the same dogs on a set schedule in the woods away from the sights, sounds, and commotion of the city.

Apollo, Big Brown, and Brian.

Photo by Mary Kay Jenkins

Then there were the Nitwits! That name was lovingly coined by their parents (Christina and Stephen), comprising Big Brown, a Chocolate Lab, and Yellow Lab littermates Apollo and Brian. Individually they were typical labs that were friendly and energetic, and the three came into the home as puppies, joining two aging Labradors and ducks! These three taught me a ton about pack mentality. When we would run as a pack, I had to be strategic about what routes to take in their neighborhood. We learned to avoid certain neighborhood streets because they would get so worked up at the sight of other dogs they could barely be held back. Often it was just curiosity and a desire to socialize, but Big Brown had a little streak of mischievousness that would rile the other two up, and chaos would rule the day! Eventually I became proactive and learned the habit of getting their attention, redirecting and pulling over to the side while giving verbal affirmation. Labradors are fantastic friends and running buddies!

Siberian Husky

Type of Runner

Huskies are some of the most athletic dogs and effortless runners around. They are a cold-weather runner's dream running buddy. They were developed to run in packs and to work on pulling loads at moderate speeds over long distances, routinely. If you are a marathoner who lives in the north or where snow is common, this is your training partner. They can do the mileage you need to train and carry a pack for your hydration and food. Whether you are fast or slow, they can handle it all, and with a smile.

They tend to gallop or bound when they run with a purposeful stride that drives them forward. Trail runners would also do well with these dogs. But the downside to their excellence in the cold is that they struggle with the heat and humidity. Their thick coat makes it hard for them to regulate internal body temperatures during the warmer months. They can be a bit aloof with other dogs, but pair them with another Husky and they gravitate toward each other and get along well. If you're going to run with one Husky, you might as well make it two!

Best suited for: Cold-weather runs | Long-distance runs at moderate pace

About

Huskies are loyal, mischievous, and outgoing. They have almond-shaped eyes that can be brown, blue, or heterochromatic with one of each. Like many of the other dogs in this chapter, regular daily exercise is important for them, mentally and physically. When it comes to capacity for work, they are definitely at the head of the class. One of the most famous races, the Iditarod, is where the Husky gets to flex his muscles. Pun only partially intended. The Alaskan race is a little over one thousand miles long and is, in my opinion, the ultimate test for the endurance and capacity of dogs. Not only is the mileage incredible, but they are tested by the conditions from whiteout blizzards to 100 degree Fahrenheit temperatures.

They are very familial and get high marks for all-around friendliness with both people and other Huskies. Unlike most of the pups on this list, they aren't the easiest to train. This has little to do with intelligence and more to do with aloofness to small tasks. If the job is to run a thousand miles, the Husky is your dog. But the rollover, play dead, and other games aren't really their jam. They can do them; they just may not want to when you ask. They have a sense for adventure and exploration, so keeping them on leash is important.

My Experience

I've run with a number of Huskies, and all of them have been amazing running partners. Diesel came to us from California; he was accustomed to the dry, breezy west-coast weather and moving to muggy Washington, DC, was a shock to the senses for sure. We had to bring him on slowly to let him acclimate to the thickness of the warmer air. Eventually, he became a fantastic running buddy who was always happy to see me. We would time shift his warm-weather runs to the morning to take advantage of the somewhat cooler air. He really made friends with every dog he ran with, even the ones who weren't so friendly. He and I really hit it off and any chance I got, I would pair him up with our girl Husky, Scout.

Scout may have the biggest personality of anyone we run with. Any photo of her really reflects her interest level in having her photo taken—zero. At best we can catch her in a moment unaware, but once she notices you, she's over it! As a runner, she eats long runs like Tic Tacs. Even the warm weather doesn't seem to wear her out. She's pretty calm and laid back by nature so maybe it's just that I can't notice a change from "regular" to "tired" Scout. She lives right next to Rock Creek Park, which is a beautiful, mostly undeveloped park in the heart of NW Washington, DC. Because of this, we spend time exclusively under the canopy of trees and on soft surfaces. Given the Husky's desire for exploration, this park offers her the opportunity to dip a toe into nature a few times a week.

Bryan and Diesel during pack pickups in the Kalorama neighborhood in Washington, DC.

Leaving a home after a dropoff.

Photo by Chris Roden

CHAPTER TEN:
Finding and Working with a Dog Runner

We have talked about all of the ways to make running with your dog a more pleasant experience, from using gear to making a running program. But, what if you aren't a runner? That's OK; not everyone who has a dog that needs to run likes to run or has the time to devote to running with their dog. We started our company six years ago because we saw a real need for hyperactive dogs to get the exercise they clearly desired and needed. We felt that there was a niche market that could benefit from a specialized service like ours. Going out for daily runs satisfies dogs in ways that three regular walks a day just cannot. There is absolutely a place and need for walks, which is why there is such a robust market for dog-walking services. We love them and the problems they help solve. But there are just some families that do not have a runner in the family, or in most cases do not have the time in their day and lives to go for consistent long runs. And even some who are fantastic runners but end up with training plans that make it next to logistically impossible to focus on their dog for those miles. We are here for you! I'd like to share a few stories of special cases where families found a service like ours to be the best fit for them.

Providing an Honest Assessment

Lentil is without question the most capable runner that has ever gone with DC Dog Runner on a run. I have spent more time and run more miles with this girl than any other dog, bar none. She's medium sized and one part hound dog and one part terminator. I say that jokingly, but I cannot think of one instance of her laying down to rest after our runs. She began running on a Monday-Wednesday-Friday schedule following our suggested day of rest to recuperate. After a few months of that and building up stamina and strength, she began picking up extra runs on off-days until she built up to running one hour each day, Monday through Friday. Browsing our social media will tell you as much, it's like searching a *Where's Waldo* book only with a brown and black dog hidden, scattered among the dirt trails, trees, and other dogs. Her owners (Dan and Julia) are young and active, so Lentil had become accustomed to early wake-up calls for morning miles. Their schedule changes required that they find another solution to her seemingly endless fountain of energy.

The single most helpful thing an owner can do when trying to find a runner to fit with their dog is to offer an honest assessment. This family presented a fantastic understanding of not only Lentil's physical needs, but her mental challenges, as well. Lentil is a bit neurotic and idles in "Back off!" They painted a great picture of a dog who was fiercely loyal and protective of her loved ones. They were also aware that the sensitivity setting on who potential threats are was high. Naturally they were cautious during the meeting at their home. I was able to set Lentil at ease because I have a natural respect for the subordinate relationship of dogs to humans. I never lose sight of that and maintain confidence that they understand and usually respond well, too.

We've tried three other runners with Lentil, two weren't a good fit, and two of us were. When searching for your dog's runner, knowing that it really is a relationship you are building will help you understand what is and is not working. Some dogs take to anyone and can hammer out miles, but most require a steady, confident hand that will lead them on a run. And in my opinion, this is a great thing, otherwise I'd be put out of business by a treadmill.

The key to remember with a dog that has special needs because of temperament challenges is to be patient and work to find the right fit for her and your family. Lentil took to me very naturally and my no-nonsense approach. I conveyed there was a task at hand (running five to six miles) and she complied. It's also helpful to note that it's not always a linear path to success. We tried a couple runners that weren't the fit for Lentil so we admitted our shortcomings and switched to something that did work. They have another dog, Mo, who is not a runner. Rather than try to build him up and try to run them as a pair, we understand that we aren't the service he needs, so he spends his time going with a wonderful company that takes him on long, slow walks around the park.

Bryan with Lentil running over a bridge in Rock Creek Park.
Photo by Chris Roden

Exercising Patience

Bear is a beautiful English Cream Retriever and comes from a lively home that loves the exercise and also the socialization our service provides. Bear's mom, Carol, would take him to the park daily to run around freely with the other neighborhood dogs on a patch of grass near the school that was an unofficial off-leash dog park around dusk. As a puppy, Bear played well, but as he grew, his play became a little too aggressive for some of the other patrons. Their situation changed and his family wanted to ensure he kept an active element to his day that would also provide the opportunity to spend time with other dogs. Dog walks and daycare only solved half the equation.

Carol called me eager to sign him up for daily hour-long runs. I admitted that we offered daily runs but that I was concerned about running with him that frequently and for that duration. Bear was still younger than two years old, so doing that kind of impactful running from a base of zero miles to six miles daily would have been too much stress on his muscular and cardiovascular systems. Ultimately we settled on three thirty-minute runs per week to start, and over a year that grew to Monday through Saturday runs. Bear was given the chance to grow into the service, and because of that, he has remained injury free. He is a strong runner that has gone from rambunctious adolescent dog to a steady focused runner that helps keep other dogs on task.

I highlight this story to show that your desires for your dog and his needs may not always line up, and that finding a professional can lead to successful, long lasting results. Bear has now been running with us for three years with no sign of slowing down.

Washington, DC, closes part of Rock Creek Parkway on Saturdays and opens it to cyclists and runners. Heidi, Scout, Bear, Beckett, and Sam.

Collaborating for Success

Sam is an athletic Black Mouth Cur who came to us looking for sorely needed exercise. He has a penchant for slipping his collar and escaping his crate to get loose. This was another example of getting a clear and honest assessment of the challenges facing the family, and how they hoped to solve them. In addition to trying to flee his wonderful home, Sam, who loves people and dogs alike, had a tendency to ignore personal space of visitors and would jump up to greet them.

To solve for this we really followed the lead of Jean and Steven, Sam's owners. They gave instructions about his leash setup, which is a prong collar plus a slip collar for reinforcement, and various other information. Since Sam is crate-trained, we let him out and put him back in on our run days to establish a routine and help him feel comfortable. And finally, to avoid bad habits, we did not allow Sam to jump on our runners. To that end we were helpful in recommending the Kong Traffic Leash that he still uses daily, and taught proper technique for changing direction to reduce pulling. We also talked about the tendency of some dogs to pull on the walk portion of the runs but that the behavior quickly melts away once the run starts. This is due to the excitement of the upcoming activity and the dogs wanting to get to it as soon as possible. With Sam, we begin runs with a warm-up walk to help shake out all the nerves and use the restroom. All of that has come together in concert to keep him running strong as well as curbing his pulling and jumping up, and it has been a great outcome for all involved.

Building Relationships

Courtney called us and wanted to know how her dog Oskar could get involved. He was a capable runner but didn't always have the motivation. He's a homebody that enjoys a plush bed or comfortable couch and has the undivided attention of a fantastic mom. He also has the attitude of a curmudgeonly old man with a face to match, even though he wasn't that old when we began running!

This family was happy to get a run in, but more than anything, wanted socialization for Oskar once a week. Relative to where I lived, he was in a far-reaching corner of "The District" and we had sparse coverage at the time because we were still a young company. I was just so motivated by someone who truly loved and valued our company that I took it as an opportunity to plant a flag on Capitol Hill and begin recruiting other dogs. We were rewarded with a well-connected dog who has Instagram credibility (@oskar.hamilton) that was willing to shout our name from the mountain tops! So I took him out every Friday for the first six months of the relationship, and then we found Gwynne! She has the proximity and patience to let Oskar be Oskar. As of the writing of this sentence in 2020, they are the cover photo for the DC Dog Runner website. It is an epic photo shot on East Capitol Street with the Capitol Building as the backdrop.

Oskar Hamilton all smiles on the brick sidewalk in Capitol Hill.

I wanted to highlight this story to show that yes, ultimately, we are taking care of dogs and their physical and mental health, but we are also providing a valuable service to someone we can bring peace of mind to. They know that our team is going to love their dog as much as they do. Sometimes that means pushing the pace and running for three miles, and other times that means taking it a little slower and stopping for breaks to use the restroom and marking things. We are a dog-running company, but we are in the business of making people and dogs happy!

There are dozens more dogs we have helped with their own unique stories that could fill the pages of a book on their own, but highlighting these few and how we helped was important in showing that as a company, we have a service and approach that shows competence through experience and continued learning. I've continued to stress "fit" throughout this book, and in some instances finding the "fit" has meant that there are some dogs we don't run. Setting the expectation with new prospective families is a much easier task six years into the life of a company. Through experience I've learned how to solve the puzzle of the owner's request, the dog's needs, the logistics of the run, and our company's capacity to deliver. Sometimes having the strength to ask a family to hold off beginning service or helping them find an alternative solution, even if that means another company, is the right call. It is not about our desire to run with every dog in Washington, DC, but rather assisting families and dogs in getting the help they need.

Questions to Ask

We recognize that many of you may not live in or around the Washington, DC, area, but there are a number of fabulous companies around the country we have talked with and learned from! I'd suggest you start with them if one is near you.

Now, what to do if you aren't near any of the companies we've highlighted? Well, let's go through a list of specifics to ask your dog-running professional. Trusting someone with your dog is like finding

177

a good babysitter for a child. There certainly are core competencies that they should have to provide safe service, but also, spend enough time with them on the phone and in person to make a confident decision.

It's helpful to remember that there are no right answers to these, but only answers that help give you a complete picture of the person and company:

1. How long have you been in service?
2. How many dogs do you currently run?
3. Do you provide solo runs, pack runs, or both?
4. How long are the runs (distance/duration)?
5. What is your policy on weather? Do you run in the rain, snow, etc.?
6. Where do you run?
7. Do you work with aggressive dogs?
8. What do you do when the dogs do not get along?
9. Does your company have insurance?
10. What is your cancellation policy?
11. Will you be running the dogs, or someone on your team? If it is someone on your team, will I be able to meet them beforehand?
12. How do we handle access to the home?
13. What do you do in the event that one of the dogs gets injured?
14. What happens if my dog is attacked by another dog? What happens if my dog bites another dog or person?
15. How do you evaluate my dog's fitness?

Depending on the maturity of the company, they may or may not have the answers to each of these questions, and that is OK. How they respond to not knowing the answer to the question you ask will give you valuable information, too. Honesty is what you are truly evaluating in their answers. It is vital to remember that the goal of this conversation is to gather as many points of information about a company and person to help you make an informed decision. This person will be responsible for caring for your family member and will have access to your home!

Being intentional about your approach to dog running, whether you or someone else will be the primary runner, will always yield the best results. Take the time and make the decision based on what is best for your dog. The only thing left to do is put down this book, lace up your shoes, grab the right gear, and take your dog for a run!

Bryan with Beckett and windswept hair.